9-8-69

WEALTH

WEALTH

AN ESSAY ON THE PURPOSES OF ECONOMICS

BY

CHARLES CARTER

VICE CHANCELLOR OF
THE UNIVERSITY OF LANCASTER

Basic Books, Inc., Publishers

NEW YORK

First published by C. A. Watts & Co. Ltd
in "The New Thinker's Library,"
General Editor: Raymond Williams
© 1968 by Charles Carter
Library of Congress Catalog Card Number: 70–93692
Printed in the United States of America

PREFACE

THE text for this book might appropriately be taken from one of Keynes's *Essays in Persuasion*—

> But, chiefly, do not let us overestimate the importance of the economic problem, or sacrifice to its supposed necessities other matters of greater and more permanent significance. It should be a matter for specialists—like dentistry. If economists could manage to get themselves thought of as humble, competent people, on a level with dentists, that would be splendid!

It occurred to me that it might assist humility if people could be encouraged to think more exactly, not just about the statistical measures of wealth, but about the purposes which that wealth serves. I am aware that in attempting to provide this encouragement I am in danger of attack from scholars of several different disciplines. As J. K. Galbraith says—

> The pursuit of happiness is admirable as a social goal. But the notion of happiness lacks philosophical exactitude; there is agreement neither on its substance nor its source. We know that it is "a profound instinctive union with the stream of life" (Bertrand Russell), but we do not know what is united. . . . Precision in scholarly discourse not only serves as an aid in the communication of ideas, but it acts

to eliminate unwelcome currents of thought, for these can almost invariably be dismissed as imprecise.

So he would class me among those who "could easily be accused of substituting for the crude economic goals of the people at large the more sensitive and refined but irrelevant goals of their own. The accusation is fatal."

Let it be so. The purpose of this book is, by discussing various aspects of Wealth, to stimulate thought; and this can be achieved even if the reader disagrees with what I say or is annoyed by its imprecision or lack of comprehensiveness. The disagreement or annoyance must be directed to me alone, for I have sought no help in writing the book, thinking it best that it should stand as an expression of a personal view. Therefore my acknowledgements can only be in a general form: thanks to all those who have moulded my present opinions, and especially to the great among the economists.

The University of Lancaster   CHARLES F. CARTER

CONTENTS

vii

I

WHAT DO WE REALLY KNOW?

THE word "wealth" has gradually been changing its meaning. It was once a general term for the goods and services which confer material well-being—whether considered as a *flow*, produced and consumed, or as a *stock* gathered in time of plenty and held to provide future benefits. It is in this general sense that Adam Smith wrote of the "Wealth of Nations". But the word has been corrupted by association with its derivation "wealthy", and now tends to be used to mean "material well-being beyond the ordinary", especially as this is provided by a large store of money, titles to money, or goods. This, however, is not a book about the rich. I have deliberately chosen in the title to use the word "wealth" in a comprehensive sense, because it is convenient to bring together the aspects of well-being which are conferred by the flow (or income) and the stock (or capital) of material things; but also because the word conveniently carries the mind forward to thoughts of "well-being" or "welfare", which are the substance of the book.

Although economics, as a subject, can trace its origins back several centuries, its main professional development is very recent, and has followed a rapidly rising curve. In 1914 the worldwide membership of the Royal Economic

Society was 694: in 1967 it was nearly 7,600, but this measure probably much understates the increase in the number of professional economists. In recent times, a large part of the interest of the profession has been devoted to the twin subjects of "development" and "growth". The first is concerned with the process by which poor countries become richer. It is a matter of some dispute as to how, historically, this process worked for the countries now relatively rich, but this has not prevented the economists of those countries from offering mountains of advice to the underdeveloped world. The second subject, "growth", is mainly theoretical and is concerned with the way in which the interrelations of economic magnitudes may affect the actual or feasible growth rate of the income of a country. Though some attention has been given to applications of growth theory to the actual increase of a rate of growth, it cannot be claimed that there has been much practical outcome.

These preoccupations of a rapidly growing profession are both concerned with "wealth": with the maximization of material well-being, whether this is broadly expressed by a measure such as national income, or in detail by an examination of the incomes of particular groups in the community: and with the maximization of the *increase* of material well-being, subject to certain constraints to prevent violent fluctuations. It is therefore very important to think clearly, not just about the particular magnitudes being maximized, but about the purposes which lie behind the whole operation. Two kinds of clear thinking are needed. One is about the measurement of material well-being; for, as so often happens in the social sciences, the measures which are available have a somewhat distant and imperfect relationship to what we really want to measure. The apparent precision of a figure has a hypnotic effect, leading the subject to forget what he is actually measuring. Thus, those who conduct examinations will spend long hours arguing whether a candidate has thirty-nine per cent, and fails, or forty per cent, and passes, and at the end will quite have forgotten that the method of examination is incapable of making a distinction as small as one per cent, and (more importantly) that it has an extremely distant relation to the qualities which the examiners believe they are measuring. So likewise, if we are told that the country's industrial production has gone up two points, we feel richer: while the news of a fall of £50m in gold and convertible currency reserves makes us feel poorer. The quantified result enters the mind with a force which inhibits thought about its true relevance.

But even if we had good and reliable indicators of material well-being, it would still be necessary to ask why it is desirable to plan its increase. The argument usually runs on the lines set out by Professor A. C. Pigou in *The Economics of Welfare*. His term "economic welfare" is defined on page 24 below, but is intended as a measure of material well-being—

When we have ascertained the effect of any cause on economic welfare, we may, unless, of course, there is specific evidence to the contrary, regard this effect as *probably* equivalent in direction, though not in magnitude, to the effect on total welfare . . . In short, there is a pre-sumption—what Edgeworth calls an "unverified prob-ability"—that qualitative conclusions about the effect of an economic cause upon economic welfare will hold good also of the effect on total welfare.

What "total welfare" means is a matter for philosophical dispute. If it is interpreted as a sum of states of individual happiness, then it is by no means obvious that in a com-munity which has attained a certain minimum level of material well-being, an increase in wealth (even of all its members) necessarily increases happiness. Why should it be assumed that the inhabitants of a rich Californian township will have their "total welfare" increased by becoming richer still? There is here, at least, a question for discussion.

Although it need not necessarily be so defined, there is a danger that the word "happiness" will carry an implica-tion of satisfaction enjoyed at the present moment, with-out consideration of its effect on other people and other times. Some may therefore prefer to define as the great end of economic effort the *improvement of the quality of civilization*. This improvement occurs when those pre-viously oppressed by poverty are set free by having enough for their needs: thus far, an increase in economic welfare implies an increase in total welfare. This, in fact, takes matters a long way, for most of mankind lives in poverty which limits the quality of civilization, and a considerable part of economic effort is concerned with the alleviation of that poverty. As Marshall wrote, "the study of the causes of poverty is the study of the cause of the degradation of a large part of mankind". But if we mean by "quality of civilization" something which can be recognized as worthy to endure and to be remembered, something which yields the happiness of great achievement, then it is far from clear that an increase in wealth of those already above the minimum will improve that quality. Here, again, is at least a subject for discussion. There has been talk in Britain of doubling the standard of living in twenty-five years, and it is generally regarded as self-evident that this is a desirable thing to do. But ought we not to think carefully in what sense welfare will be greater as a consequence, and whether we can influence the nature or distribution of the extra production so that desirable changes in total welfare will be made likely, and bad ones minimized?

This is not a philosophical treatise. I have no doubt that the philosophers could do much to require from the economists clearer thinking about the purpose of producing wealth, but I must not attempt to ape their professional competence. It seemed worth while, however, for an economist to spend the pages of a small book in discussing some of the implications of the word "wealth", in the hope thereby of stimulating others to think more accurately on issues which are important in everyday decisions. In the rest of this chapter, I give some examples which may at least serve to undermine the reader's confidence that statements about "growth" or "wealth", or the terms "richer" and "poorer" (applied to communities), have a firm and self-evident meaning. Chapter II touches lightly on the work of a few economic thinkers,

for I need to explain why the profession has shown a
certain inadequacy in relating its analysis to a clear ultimate
purpose; but a single chapter is, of course, far from
enough to provide a representative sample of what
economists have written on the matter. Then a series of
short chapters picks up particular aspects of the study of
wealth: the effect of *time* and *uncertainty*: differences between short- and long-run satisfactions: the relation of
"paper" to "real" wealth: the effect of knowing what our
neighbours possess: the consequences of our knowledge
of partial and imperfect indicators of wealth. The argument is then pulled together in two chapters, one about
wealth and individual happiness, and one about wealth
and the quality of civilization. From these there arise some
practical considerations which are set out in the last chapter.

A man who has twenty pounds is better off than a man
who has ten. So much appears obvious: and statements
which are obvious deserve a cautious examination, in case
they prove to be meaningless. In fact, it is easy to con-
struct many reasons why the man with twenty pounds
might be (in some reasonable sense) the worse off of the
two. For instance, he might have six children, and the
other man none; or the twenty pounds might have to
last a month, and the ten only a week. Furthermore, the
sense of being "better off" is relative to some expectation:
Dives, with twenty pounds in his pocket, would feel
worse off than Lazarus with ten. Or is even that a
meaningful statement? Can we ever compare the state of

well-being of two different human beings? Or even of the same person, at two different times?

Meaningful or not, comparisons are often made. The American engineer is three times as well off as his British counterpart: hence the flight of trained manpower across the Atlantic. Sweden was thirty-five per cent richer than Britain: British income per head is more than half as large again as that in the Irish Republic: the richest countries in the world are twenty times as well off as the poorest: in the "league table" of economic welfare Britain has slipped behind France and West Germany. Statements like these are common in the Press and in the speeches of experts. Furthermore, the vast literature— academic and popular, practical and theoretical—about economic growth presupposes the existence of something definite which is supposed to grow.

When the economic growth or relative success of nations is being discussed, the measure being used is commonly the national product or national income. *The gross domestic product at market prices* is the sum of the values of all the goods and services produced in a country: the *gross national product* adds to this the income received from overseas (that is to say, the *net* balance of the inward and outward flows of such things as property income): *the gross national product at factor cost* is found by subtracting the part of the market value of goods and services which is simply due to taxes (such as the petrol tax), and adding back the amount of subsidies: the (net) *national income* is the part of the gross national product at factor cost which is left over after setting aside enough to replace worn-out items of equipment. The gross domestic product is a measure of the producing power of a country, considered as a giant factory; the national income measures what the inhabitants of a country can safely consume without affecting future prosperity—that is, without "living on their fat".

There are of course many statistical difficulties in measuring quantities like these. The figures are necessarily inaccurate, and necessarily somewhat out of date. But the real difficulties come, not from inaccuracy, but from the limits (often unnoticed) on what is measured. First, the measure is normally of the product or income of a country in terms of the prices of that country. How, then, is one to compare figures from two different countries? An easy way out is to use an official rate of exchange between currencies, say \$2.40 = £1, but a rate of exchange is usually an artificial and manipulated ratio, and its use makes it extremely difficult to give any clear meaning to the comparison. A more sophisticated way is to estimate in the prices of both countries, and make two comparisons: for instance, to try to compute the United States gross product at British prices, comparing it (in pounds sterling) with the British gross product, and also the British product at US prices, comparing it (in dollars) with the US product. Thus we get two ratios, and can either quote both or rely on the principle (which has some slender justification) that Truth will lie somewhere in between the two answers.

These double comparisons may yield tiresome results; for instance, it may be possible to show that incomes at *A* are higher than at *B*, and (with equal justification) that incomes at *B* are higher than at *A*. More important, however, is the fact that the comparison proposed may be impossible, simply because some of the things produced or consumed do not exist in both countries. It is said (though I fear that the story may be apocryphal) that Mr. Henry Ford, desiring to compare the purchasing power of wages in different countries, filled a hamper with the clothes of a typical American automobile worker and sent it to various countries for the contents to be priced. In due course it arrived in Dublin, and was taken to a suitable tailor. He lifted the lid of the hamper, turned over the contents, shook his head sadly, and said "No decent Dublin working man would be seen dead in such clothes". Plainly what is difficult in a comparison of Dublin with Detroit becomes even more doubtful or impossible if London is to be compared with Calcutta; and the difficulties which attend comparisons between countries or regions with different needs and habits also apply to comparisons between people or social groups of widely different incomes or modes of living.

Another problem arises from the need to make arbitrary decisions about what is to be included in the national product. Generally speaking, production is included if its output is bought and sold, or could without violence to the social customs of the country be bought and sold. Thus, in the British statistics, the costs of the National Health Service (and of many other services provided free by public authorities) are included as a value of production, because, although these services are not in fact bought by the user, there is no reason of principle why they could not be. The owner-occupier of a house is assumed to pay himself an imaginary rent, which is included in the national product; if this were not done, the national product would go down every time a tenant bought his house, which would be a curious anomaly.

It is obviously desirable that any internationally accepted set of definitions, for use in drawing up statistical tables, should be as inclusive as possible of kinds of production which are bought and sold in some countries but not in all, or (within a country) in some circumstances but not in all. There must at least be a clear rule, to include or exclude. Unfortunately, however, it is hard to be logical on these matters. Domestic service is bought and sold in most countries, but the service performed by housewives within the family is excluded, presumably on the grounds that, since husband and wife are "one flesh", the husband ought not to be deemed to pay his wife. Her clothes and food are a free gift, and she freely gives her services in the kitchen.

Suppose two countries each have fifty million people, and a national product (on the normal definition) of £40,000m (i.e. £800 per head); but one country has larger families than the other, so that it contains ten million housewives whose work (at market rates) is worth £600 a year on the average, while the other contains fifteen million housewives, with fewer children to feed but more spacious houses to care for, doing work of average value £500. Then the inclusion of the work of housewives would raise the product of the first country to £46,000m (£920 per head), but that of the second country to £47,500m (£950 per head). The difference corresponds to a real fact, namely that the second country is able to enjoy a higher standard of housewifery (per head); but it is a difference which is not revealed by the normal presentation of the figures.

If comparisons are attempted with countries with a very different social structure, more difficult questions may arise. We have almost forgotten in Britain the days when a bride of a good family was accompanied by a dowry—a payment which perhaps expressed the fact that women of good family were regarded as an economic liability to their husbands. But in some parts of Africa a bride, who may be expected to take a large share of work in the fields as well as to bring up the family, is unequivocally an economic asset, and is normally the subject of a bride payment to her family, which is losing the advantage of her services. (In some places, this payment may be refunded if she does not suit!) If a bride has a capital value, it is anomalous to assume that her daily services are given free. It would be like ignoring the contribution to production made by a slave, because he receives no wage.

You may well think by now that a simple way through all these difficulties is to include every activity which demonstrably contributes to human welfare—perhaps with a few exclusions of convenience, such as sexual relations (although they have for thousands of years had a market price). But this leads us to the most serious difficulty of all. In any rich and complex society, a great deal of the work done—and duly counted in the flow of

wealth produced—is simply required to offset the disadvantages of living in a rich and complex society. Thus
we count, as part of our production, both the cost of
running cars, and the cost of traffic management to overcome the consequent congestion of the roads—as well as
the cost of ambulance or hospital services to deal with the
resultant accidents. We count both the production of
cigarettes, and the services of chest surgeons to operate
for lung cancer. The cost of a given level of public
administration may go up as a community becomes more
complex—for instance, its tax system will probably be
more elaborate; but tax inspectors, even though from the
point of view of the community they are no more than a
regrettable necessity, are counted in the national product
as though they made an independent contribution to welfare. Most important of all, national defence is treated as
having a value equal to its cost, and nations appear to
get richer simply because (as a response to the actions of
their rivals) they have been engaging in rearmament.

The result of all this is that we have a built-in tendency
to exaggerate the welfare significance of differences between rich and poor countries. In 1965, national income
per head in Britain was about £525, while in the Republic
of Ireland it was only £285. But there would have been
no sense at all in Ireland's trying to match our level of
defence expenditure per head: she is too small to mount
an independent defence, and the limit of her requirements
is therefore a "police force" for internal security and
something to contribute to United Nations forces. If we
ignore defence as part of the production of both countries,

incomes per head become about £485 and £280. But at least £2,000m (and perhaps much more) of British income must be simply performing the service of overcoming problems which Ireland, a simpler and less densely settled country, does not have. From the point of view of a comparison of welfare, income figures of £450 and £280 per head may thus be more relevant; in other words, it may be more sensible to say that the Irish are about sixty-two per cent as well off as we are, rather than fifty-four per cent given by the crude figures. And even this, as we shall see in later chapters, does not take us far enough.

A similar difficulty arises from genuine differences in human needs in different places—the most obvious example of which is the need for heat and warm clothing in cold countries, and for superior hygiene and medical services in tropical countries. About £2,500m, or eight per cent, of British production would not be needed if the average temperature was 18°C all the year round. Countries plainly differ greatly in the natural obstacles (of distance, lifting over hills and mountains, controlling seas and rivers) which they have to overcome; and this again introduces an uncertainty into judgements of welfare.

Statistics thus give a spurious precision to our thinking about the wealth and welfare of nations and people. But, even if we take them at their face value, it is important to think precisely about what they are saying. Consider, for instance, that well-established fact, the disappointing trend of British productivity in recent years. From 1956 to 1966 the gross domestic product, measured at constant prices so as to eliminate the effect of price changes, went up by a little under thirty-five per cent. During this period the working population rose by only about four per cent, so that the product per worker per year rose by nearly thirty per cent. Hours actually worked are not known for all types of worker, but hours per week actually worked by operatives in manufacturing industries fell by six per cent, and hours worked by all full-time manual workers by about five and a half per cent. (The standard working week fell by more than this, but the average amount of overtime has gone up.) Furthermore, the length of holidays has probably increased; consequently it is reasonable to suppose that, over all workers, the fall in hours worked in the *year* was at least six per cent. The rise in product per worker per hour was thus about thirty-seven per cent. The total population of Britain has been increasing faster than the working population, so the product available per consumer has not risen as fast as the product per worker. But in making comparisons with other countries the various elements of this calculation will be different. Some countries have sustained a rapid increase in production by drawing on large reserves of labour. Some show a different trend of hours worked. Furthermore, we must be careful not to assume without discussion that a lessening of production, caused by shorter hours worked, is evidence of failure. (The reduction in question is not in the zone in which a shortening of hours could be expected so to lessen fatigue as to lead to a compensating increase in production per hour.) The shorter hours were not forced by economic circumstances on an unwilling labour force; there was a choice, in favour of shorter hours and more leisure, rather than more production. Thus the record of Britain over the ten years is that of increasing production by thirty-five per cent *and* obtaining the benefits of greater leisure, and it is misleading to judge this performance in terms of the material product alone.

There is nothing in the examples just given which is not well known to national-income statisticians. The problem is rather that, once figures are written on paper, the qualifications which should attach to their use are quickly forgotten. The need for precise thinking relates, not only to the meaning of the available figures but also to their relation to the fundamental purposes of economic activity.

There are analogous problems when we try to classify areas of the world as "rich" or "poor", not in current income, but in their resources. The wealth of a region is not something which can be measured in isolation, forgetting the people who dwell there. Oils or metals which are in a totally inaccessible place have no value. If the cost of winning them and taking them to places where they can reasonably be used would be very high, so that neither now nor in the foreseeable future would they be worth exploitation, they might as well not exist. But a resource which is valueless at one time may obtain a value because of the growth of population nearby, or the opening up of new communications, or because of some technical or political change which affects its marketability. A country at war, cut off from normal sources of supply, may suddenly discover a value in resources which previously were considered valueless.

The wealth of a country or region is therefore a function, not only of quantities of natural resources, but of the relation of these resources to possible markets. Indeed, the whole structure of the economy which exploits and uses the resources is relevant. A remark such as that "Britain is trying to maintain a large population at a high standard of living on a small and poor island" (which I have often made myself) does not have any clear meaning. Great Britain is "poor" in the sense of having a fairly narrow *range* of large-scale natural resources (though she has small quantities of many minerals); but the mere fact of being small and heavily populated means that her resources are well placed in relation to those who use them. For instance, our cities are surrounded by fertile and well-watered agricultural land. The meaning of the word "poor", applied to a country like Britain, becomes even more obscure if one reflects that the population of a country is itself one of its natural resources, which has been improved by education and training. Also, the geographical position of a country can be in itself a form of "wealth"; Britain derives advantage from her easy sea communications, and from her position close to routes linking Europe and America.

I hope that by this point I have induced in the reader a

certain caution in making remarks about the wealth of nations. As will repeatedly appear in the later chapters, the same caution is needed in talking about the wealth of individuals. We have always to keep in mind that the effect of the increase of a country's income on the satisfaction of its inhabitants depends on how the income is distributed. In our time, the extreme example is provided by the riches of some of the sheikhdoms of the Persian Gulf, which have largely remained with the ruling families. There is no natural law that increases in the flow of wealth will tend to reduce inequalities. A country (or a world) which is becoming richer can more easily arrange to reduce inequality, if it wishes, for it is possible to help the poor from the increasing income without taking away from the rich. But there are plenty of cases in which this reduction of inequality fails to happen— indeed, taking the world as a whole, it is possible that inequality may be increasing.

As we shall see in more detail in Chapter VI, the satisfaction derived from a certain flow of wealth is in part *relative*, both to expectations and to what is happening to others in the community. It is therefore possible that a country might be becoming richer, but the level of satisfaction of the majority of its citizens might be falling —both because they see a few people becoming very wealthy, and because (though not actually poorer) they feel cheated of reasonable expectations.

Before concluding that a person who has received a larger flow of wealth is in consequence likely to be "happier" or "more satisfied" (or, in more neutral language, to have "moved to a preferred position"), it is necessary to inquire whether other things have remained equal. A part of our wealth is needed to overcome the disadvantages of our environment, and these disadvantages may vary. For instance, in a cold winter the contribution to national production of the coal, gas and electricity industries will go up. The flow of wealth increases, and certain money incomes will rise. But all this is used simply to keep no warmer than one would have kept in a mild winter; an apparent increase in wealth can exist side by side with a decline in the satisfaction of the majority of citizens (except for those few who revel in fighting the worst that the climate can achieve). This is an example of expenditure on what has been called a "regrettable necessity"—that is, something which might conceivably, at a happier time or place, be avoided, but is unavoidable here and now. With fuel for cold weather we can class the services of tax inspectors and the C.I.D., breathalysers, casualty wards in hospitals—all examples of goods and services which cannot be said to yield positive enjoyment, but prevent our decline into a less satisfactory state.

The leading example of something accepted by the majority as a "regrettable necessity" is the service of the Armed Forces. Although to some rulers (for instance, Hitler) an army may give a certain pleasure, being an instrument for achieving one's will by aggression, to the great majority of citizens the benefit received from the armed forces is simply a feeling of safety. This feeling is a consequence, not of the absolute level of military preparation, but of the relative state of the armaments of one's own country (together with those of any reliable allies) in relation to the armaments of a potential aggressor or rival. Arms expenditure therefore shares with advertising (see page 65) the peculiar property that it can escalate, and everyone will feel worse off; for the balance of military power may be just where it was before, but the greater quantity and sophistication of armaments increase the fear that war may break out by accident, and the burden of expenditure is more onerous.

A country will be counted richer by the national-income statisticians if it produces more atomic warheads, tanks or napalm. Spending on arms is a major interest of the great powers, and the fluctuations of that spending from year to year may be considerable, even in times of nominal peace. Here, therefore, is an important situation in which an apparent increase in the flow of wealth may involve a decline in the satisfaction of nearly all citizens. Arms races can provide a combination of increasing prosperity with increasing unhappiness. Indeed, war itself may be consistent with a high civilian standard of living, as the example of the United States in the Second World War shows; but no one argues that wars are desirable on this account. We have to be careful in drawing conclusions about wealth wherever the figures are distorted by the influence of military spending.

II

THE ECONOMISTS' VIEW OF WEALTH AND WELFARE

To the very first page of Adam Smith's *Wealth of Nations*, J. R. McCulloch added a footnote pointing out that "Dr. Smith has not stated the precise meaning he attached to the term *wealth*; though he most commonly describes it as the 'annual produce of land and labour'." To this McCulloch objects, on the grounds that it would include all the useless products of the earth, and he proposes to define wealth "as comprising all the articles or products that are necessary, useful or agreeable to man, and which at the same time possess exchangeable value". The discovery that "value in exchange" is a measurable concept, distinct from a subjective impression of usefulness, was an important beginning to the development of economics, but it raises problems which for long remained unperceived or unanswered. These relate in part to the definition of wealth (or income) and in part to the relation of this definition to the purposes of economics.

John Stuart Mill stated boldly, on the first page of his *Principles of Political Economy*, that "Everyone has a notion, sufficiently correct for common purposes, of what is meant by wealth". The word "everyone" here does not include the Mercantilists, for he next spends several pages disposing of the "palpable absurdity" that wealth consists solely of money or of precious metals. In the course of this demolition he discovers the relevance of that aspect of money which we now call "liquidity", and which is further mentioned on page 52 below—

> We really, and justly, look upon a person as possessing the advantages of wealth, not in proportion to the useful and agreeable things of which he is in the actual enjoyment, but to his command over the general fund of things useful and agreeable; the power he possesses of providing for any exigency, or obtaining any object of desire. Now, money is itself that power . . .[1]

Wealth is everything which has a *power of purchasing*—that is to say, money, and all things exchangeable for money or for other things. The free gifts of nature, such as air, do not form part of wealth. Mill then observes that communal and individual wealth are different—

> In the wealth of mankind, nothing is included which does not of itself answer some purpose of utility or pleasure. To an individual, anything is wealth, which, though useless in itself, enables him to claim from others a part of their stock of things useful or pleasant.

He instances the "paper wealth" of a mortgage, which cancels out when debts and credits are summed over a whole nation; and (a more interesting example) slaves, which he claims cannot be part of the world's wealth

[1] *Principles of Political Economy*, 1871 ed., p. 3.

because the capital value of free men is not counted. He thus chanced on the difficulties, familiar to national-income statisticians, of the treatment of things which have a value in exchange in part of the economy only. But the question of whether "immaterial products" were wealth he regarded as not of very great importance; and answered it by deciding that services cannot be regarded as yielding wealth, because they cannot be accumulated. This is a distinction which creates more problems than it answers, for it includes in the flow of wealth material goods (such as pints of milk and bananas) which are virtually useless for the purpose of accumulation, but on grounds of logic denies a place to the great actor or musician except as an "unproductive labourer".

Alfred Marshall's attempts at definition are no great aid to clarity. He was anxious to use words in a way conformable with ordinary business practice. He therefore defines wealth as the stock of material goods, or rights to material goods, together with immaterial goods external to the owner, and serving directly as a means of acquiring material goods—that is to say, his business goodwill. He considers it possible that one might also want to talk about "personal wealth" as including "energies, faculties and habits which directly contribute to making people industrially efficient"; and he talks about one person having "more real wealth in the broadest sense" because he has a better climate, better roads, better water, and more wholesome drainage. This leads him to a brief mention of *collective goods*, not in private ownership; but he confuses the issue by proceeding directly from man-made collective goods to the river Thames, which "has added more to the wealth of England than all its canals, and perhaps even than all its railroads".[1]

In the second edition of the *Principles*, the chapter on Wealth was linked to a chapter on Income by a paragraph which defines gross income as the flow of new elements of wealth, of benefits derived from the use of wealth, and of "such passing enjoyments as from their fleeting nature cannot be included in the stock of wealth, but yet have a market value or are commonly acquired by money payments". In later editions, the chapter on Wealth is left stranded, with no apparent relation to what follows. But it is at least clear that Marshall recognizes services as part of income, and that he sees that a problem exists in discussing the contribution of collective goods. In parentheses, it may be added that the abandonment of the earlier practice of considering wealth as a flow as well as a stock does not improve the clarity of terminology, for Marshall is now involved with the difference between real income and money income; this he made tolerably clear in the early, but not in the later editions. One of the casualties of revision was the charming example of the inclusion in the flow of wealth of the value of a service which a man might otherwise perform for himself—

In a pamphlet published in 1767 on the typical budget of a London clerk with £50 a year, who is supposed to live on the meanest food and clean his own boots, we find

[1] *Principles of Economics*, 8th ed., Book II, Chapter II.

entered a weekly item of 6d. for "Shaving, and Combing a Wig twice".

This is a reminder that definitions based on what is normally the subject of market exchange may produce odd results, particularly where comparisons over time or space are involved.

Much that Marshall failed to clarify is illuminated by the work of his successor, Pigou. In *The Economics of Welfare*, which succeeded *Wealth and Welfare* (1912), he sets up what he describes as a "rough distinction" between those aspects of welfare which are and are not the proper subject of economic inquiry. He defines as being within the scope of the economist "that part of social welfare that can be brought directly or indirectly into relation with the measuring rod of money". The word "social" is not in Pigou's original definition, and it is not clear what it implies, for at some points he appears to be discussing the welfare of individuals. The "relation with the measuring rod of money" means, of course, much more than direct marketability; thus, if it is necessary to pay a man $10,000 extra in order to persuade him to work in Alaska instead of Florida, and if it can be shown that the conditions of life other than climate will be the same in the two places, it would be possible to claim that a difference of climate has, in its effect on welfare, been measured in money terms. But this does not mean that you can buy the weather, like a commodity in a shop.

Pigou's work is basically about the size and distribution of the "national dividend", that is to say the net national product or flow of usable wealth, and the effects which both size and distribution have upon economic welfare. His interest is especially in the effects, good and bad, of various interferences, frictions and indivisibilities in the economic process—

> Certain optimistic followers of the classical economists have suggested that the "free play of self-interest", if only Government refrains from interference, will automatically cause the land, capital and labour of any country to be so distributed as to yield a larger output and, therefore, more economic welfare than could be attained by any arrangement other than that which comes about "naturally".

He deals with this view exhaustively, by taking case after case of possible divergence between the marginal social and the marginal private net product. The marginal *social* product is that which is due to a small increment of resources in a given use or place, no matter to whom any part of this product may accrue. The *private* product is that which accrues to the person or body responsible for investing the resources. Thus, if a factory emits black smoke, the product received by its owner may be greater than the social product, because he pays nothing towards the extra costs which his neighbours bear in cleaning up the dirt. The divergence in this example provides a reason for believing that economic welfare might be increased by an interference, namely smoke control, whose cost to the factory owner would be less than its benefit to the community.

The Economics of Welfare is thus a highly practical book,

bearing directly on important questions of public policy such as the control of competition, taxes, bounties, rationing and wage regulation. Unfortunately the subject now called Welfare Economics has become much concerned with the logical foundations, and at times its practitioners appear to be satisfied to have proved the logical impossibility of strong and relevant assertions about economic welfare. But decisions affecting economic welfare are the daily substance of Government, and to prove that such decisions cannot be made with precision is a profoundly useless and unhelpful act. There are many criticisms which can be made of Pigou's work, but he needs successors rather than critics.

The relation between wealth and welfare was for long discussed by the use of the concept of *utility*. This was at times thought of as a unit of pleasure or satisfaction, but, as both Marshall and Pigou pointed out, what is observable (for instance, in the actions of a purchaser) is related not to satisfaction achieved, but to desire. Men desire things which will not give them satisfaction, and fail to desire things which, once obtained, would give great satisfaction.[1] For technical reasons (whose validity is still the subject of occasional dispute) the idea of utility as a quantity in principle numerical (in the sense that "twice as much" has a meaning) has in most economic writing given way to statements about preference and indifference. Faced with commodities A, B and C, at given prices, and being told to spend his money on one of them, a purchaser shows *preference* for A over B (say),

[1] See also page 89.

but is *indifferent*, that is has no preference, where *B* and *C* are concerned. But the double movement from satisfaction to desire, and from units of desirability to statements of preference, has detached economic discussion very effectively from its origins in utilitarian philosophy. The result is that economists often seem unwilling to consider what should be a main interest of their subject, namely the relation between the stock and the flow of wealth and the satisfaction, or happiness, or state of civilization of this and of later generations.

This fact can be illustrated by referring to the most widely read of the economics textbooks, which are important in forming the views of new generations of economists about the nature of their subject. Many of them say nothing at all about the relationship of economic analysis to the satisfaction of mankind, or content themselves with a few sentences to show that they do not really believe that money measures everything relevant. Sir Alexander Cairncross does indeed spend three pages, in his *Introduction to Economics*, on wealth and welfare, wealth from the individual and social points of view, "paper" wealth, and the relation of wealth to income; but this is unusual. Sir Dennis Robertson, in his *Lectures on Economic Principles*, showed (as one would expect of that great man) a broader outlook than most—

> [Material welfare] must be conceived as a flow of enjoyment or satisfaction derived from the good things of life. But not as consisting in all the possible kinds of satisfaction. Ruskin, enraged at what he regarded as the narrow conception of wealth prevalent among the economists of a

hundred years ago, cried out in protest "There is no wealth but life." But that protest goes too far, and to act on it would make our study unmanageable. We must limit ourselves to the more material and less spiritual parts or aspects of welfare. This is admittedly a hazy boundary line...

But this outlook does little to alter the subsequent analysis in the *Lectures*.

A typical reference from a recent textbook (*A New Prospect of Economics*, written by various Liverpool authors) evades the problem as follows—

... Here ... we are only concerned with *economic* welfare ... The wider problem of movements of welfare in general —what might be called happiness—is left to the philosophers. However, most economists, following the opinion of Professor A. C. Pigou and, one can imagine, of most people other than ascetics, have suggested that the two are positively correlated. That is to say, if economic welfare increases, welfare in general will increase and vice versa. But even if this contention were denied it is still desirable to analyse the movements of the components of welfare, of which economic welfare is a significant member. (p. 409)

The authors then go on to refer to the necessity for assuming *unchanged tastes* in comparing welfare in two situations. But what if a change of tastes is a necessary or highly probable accompaniment of a movement from one situation to the other?

Even so careful a writer as Professor G. L. S. Shackle can be found taking an unwarranted step in his logic (*Economics for Pleasure*, p. 1)—

Some philosophers have thought that all ends and purposes converge upon one, and can be reduced to the pursuit of the *summum bonum*, the individual's unified, coherent conception of the good life. They have maintained, even, that only by supposing this can we account for our ability to weigh against each other our desire for a little more of this and our desire for a little more of that, an ability which, when one considers it, is quite puzzling when the things are as different as, say, music and mutton. But the economist is not really concerned with this puzzle. There is in any person's world of experience or of imagination a tremendous variety of desirable kinds of thing, plainly distinct from each other. There is also, for each person and for all of us together, a plain impossibility of getting so much of every one of these kinds, all at once, that we could not possibly find any enjoyment in having any more ... To each person by himself this impossibility presents itself as a lack of money.

There is here a concealed assumption that satisfaction is built up to higher levels by the addition of units bought with money. The observed fact that riches do not always provide satisfaction is not mentioned; it presumably has to be explained away by a change of tastes.

Younger economists seldom find it necessary even to mention that the quantities in their equations stand at one remove from the purposes which, in the other part of their life, as ordinary members of society, they would think it right for mankind to pursue. They often set out a piece of theoretical economic analysis as leading to a certain line of practical policy, when it is evident that the policy (if applied) would fail or have strongly undesirable effects. But it is not within the compass of their interests to look beyond the immediate results of formal economic analysis; this, they consider, would be to invade the area of professional competence of the philosopher, the sociologist, the political scientist, the technologist or some other specialist. Yet it cannot be expected that those who make decisions will always observe that the package received from the economist bears, in invisible ink, the label: "Do not use until you have consulted all other relevant specialists"; and I cannot believe that it is good that a subject, which began with a concern for the betterment of mankind, should be allowed to develop as a formal structure without constant examination of the relation of this structure to welfare, broadly defined.

In this book I am to some extent returning to the position of Sir Ralph Hawtrey, who in his book *The Economic Problem* (1926) argues strongly against the limitation of the economist's interest in welfare. "Economics *cannot* be dissociated from ethics", he says, and (after quoting Pigou's definition of economic welfare) he continues—

> In identifying welfare with satisfactions, Professor Pigou is implicitly assuming in the individual a disposition to prefer the greater pleasure. The former assumption is no closer approximation to the truth than the latter, and we cannot adopt it. We must reserve our freedom to say whether and to what extent any particular kind of satisfaction is to be regarded as welfare . . . (p. 184)
> . . . The consumer's preferences have a very slight relation to the real good of the things he chooses. Market value is so far

from being a true measure of ethical value that it is hardly ever a first approximation to it. We are compelled, therefore, to give up what has been from the very start the leading idea of economics, the idea of a *measurable aggregate* of economic welfare, which forms part or a constituent of welfare as a whole. The mercantilists' ideal of wealth, the classical economists' ideal of utility, Professor Pigou's "satisfaction", none of these can be legitimately so regarded . . . (p. 215)

In my copy of the book, which belonged to Keynes, this latter passage is heavily marked. As the reviewers of Hawtrey's book noted at the time, however, he is more successful in stating problems than in solving them, and his own attempts to define a leading idea for economics are not successful. My purpose in what follows is more modest: I seek only to stimulate some broader thinking about what economists should say about wealth and welfare.

III

REMEMBERING TIME

On the whole, economists have not shown a great deal of interest in the ultimate use of goods bought by private individuals. Things pass from the shelves of the shops to the "final consumer", and, because he is final (in the sense that most goods are not bought and sold again after they reach him) the use he makes of what he buys seems to be of little concern. The exceptional areas, which have been much more fully examined, are the goods for which the second-hand market is very important (automobiles provide the standard case) and the goods whose durability affects the pattern of purchases by making it possible to delay replacement. The demand for television sets can have very wide swings, and is readily affected by Government policies, such as the control of hire purchase; the demand for salt is, under all normal circumstances, much more regular and less easily controlled. Durable goods, like television sets, therefore tend to be considered with more care by those whose interest is the formation of economic policy.

If we look at wealth in its relation to enjoyment, or to the increase of civilization, it is clear at once that a purchaser does not receive a single instantaneous contribution to his welfare at the moment at which he purchases some article or service. Note first that his purchase may be enjoyable in prospect. The expectation of being able to buy some sweets next Saturday may be, to a child, more enjoyable than the sweets themselves. Many a member of the Armed Services has enjoyed in advance, in his daydreams, the purchase of a little country pub or a corner shop which he hopes to make on his discharge. The essence of *enjoyment in prospect* is that the thing to be bought must not be of a routine kind. The housewife does not enjoy in prospect the purchase of next week's supply of detergent, but she may well dream happily of a new hat.

Once obtained, goods and services yield up the quality for which they were desired over a period which ranges almost from zero to infinity. A ticket to a concert is an advance purchase of the right to enjoy sounds which die on the air almost as soon as they are made; here nearly all the true enjoyment at the time of the concert is in the cumulative effect on the senses of a succession of sounds. The rich man who gives his native town a public park may do so because he enjoys the prospect of the enjoyment of others in perpetuity. The economist must here beware of the assumption that what lies far in the future must always be discounted so much that it can be ignored. A man who builds himself a massive tomb does so, not because he enjoys the prospect of being remembered a week after his death, but because he likes the idea of *still* being remembered in a thousand years.

Between the instantaneous and the perpetual there lies the duration of enjoyment of most of our everyday purchases: the sausages, which satisfy us over a few minutes of eating and a few hours of digestion: the insurance premium, which yields the enjoyment of a certain kind of financial security for a year: the book, enjoyed over a few hours of reading, then in retrospect, then perhaps enjoyed again at a second reading or by a second reader in the household: the table, which may yield its services over centuries. Looking at this range of durability, it may seem that the rational man would be willing to pay a higher price for things which last a long time; for instance, for shoes which last two years instead of one. But the validity of this depends on the meaning given to "rationality". Human beings need not only to be fed and clothed; they need to be stimulated. The shopkeeper who offered ladies, at a high price, an everlasting hat would not sell many; for hats and other fashion goods get more and more boring as their use continues, until eventually the tedium outweighs the practical utility, and the goods are replaced even though they are not worn out.

The example of the everlasting hat illustrates another point, namely that the enjoyment to be obtained from a purchase depends on the ownership of other goods, both by the purchaser and by other people. A hat is desirable if it matches or complements an outfit; and when the outfit changes, the hat may cease to be of use. Relationships in demand go considerably beyond those normally cited in the textbooks. The purchase of a new carpet does not absolutely require the replacement of curtains or wallpaper (in the way in which the purchase of a car necessarily leads to purchases of petrol), but it can sharply reduce the enjoyment to be obtained from all the things in the room which do not "go with it". So with a hat and the clothes which are worn with it.

The enjoyment from a hat also depends, in a complicated way, on the hats worn by other women. A hat is not normally desirable if exactly the same one can be seen on many other heads. There is value in being a little different, but not too much so; a hat which is different by being quite obviously out of fashion loses value, except to a small number of people who enjoy shocking their neighbours. Thus, to make an everlasting hat a worthwhile product, the producer would have to be confident of three things: that a customer would never get bored with the hat, that she would never cease to have in her wardrobe an outfit to which the hat is appropriate, and that changes in the fashion of other people's hats would never make the everlasting hat undesirable. No one of these conditions is likely to be valid, and durability is not therefore a highly considered feature in hats. 1507782

It is customary among men to dismiss such peculiarities of the fashion market as being due to the well-known irrationality of females. In fact, however, the class of goods whose effective durability is not determined by being worn out or literally consumed is very wide. It includes, for instance, ties, the records of pop songs, magazines, and many books. The class of goods which, though they may be used until physically worn out, have their value in the meantime affected by changes of fashion is wider still. It certainly now includes automobiles: this year's shape is, in a subtle and usually quite irrational way, more to be desired than last year's shape.

Some goods have the peculiar quality that the flow of enjoyment they produce falls off over time, and then increases again. This is often true, for instance, of well-made pieces of furniture. Many families which inherited Victorian furniture were, by about 1950, heartily sick of its ponderous size and complicated shape, but at that time it was so little regarded that one might have to pay to get it removed. Many items must have been destroyed at this time which now would command a good price. This is partly, of course, a matter of fashion, but an article which has become "old enough to be interesting" is likely to continue to be desired as it gets still older.

Even when an article or a service has yielded up the last of its direct benefits, either because it is worn out or used up, or because it has become unfashionable, incompatible or out of date, it may still yield further benefits in retrospect. A hat which a woman would "not be seen dead in" today may still yield fond memories. A holiday is valued in retrospect, often more than at the time. A concert, the sight of a great work of art, the reading of great literature can give enjoyment long after the time—indeed, they may in some sense change a man and enrich him for the rest of his life. The qualities and creations which we regard as the essence of good in a civilization are in large measure those whose memory is kept green because, once appreciated, they are enjoyed in retrospect. Shakespeare is an "immortal memory".

Great commercial enterprises turn out, for us to buy, vast quantities of sensations enjoyable in the moment but then forgotten. It is important that our pursuit of wealth should not be too much concentrated on these ephemeral things.

The danger that this may be so arises because, though it is not universally true that we discount (that is reduce the importance of) a future prospect, we probably do tend to underestimate a *prospect of our own retrospective enjoyment*. This is partly because it is an ill-defined prospect, for there is pleasure to be obtained from thinking in advance of something which will occur on a definite date. One often hears people say such things as: "Three weeks from today, I shall be basking in the sun on the Spanish coast". It would not come naturally to say: "Two months from today, I shall be remembering with enjoyment my Spanish holiday", because the retrospective memory is not (such things as wedding anniversaries apart) assignable to a particular date. Two months from today, you may be looking urgently for a dentist to remove a nagging tooth, and holiday memories may be far from your thoughts.

The example applies to more important things. A splendid performance of *King Lear* may in fact recur to the memory for fifty years, and offer refreshment of spirit and an insight into greatness repeatedly in that time. But this prospect does not make it easy to sell tickets for *King Lear*, the price of which reflects the expectation of immediate enjoyment rather than the hope of great memories.

I use the word "hope" advisedly, for it may not be certain in advance of the performance that it will in fact be splendid. We are constantly buying the chance of enjoyment, rather than the certainty. Almost every book we buy is a gamble. It occasions no surprise if a new suit, once home, does not seem as attractive as it did in the shop. We buy tins of baked beans in the certainty that each will taste the same as the previous one. The manufacturer of a popular product can gain by such standardization: the certainty of a precise measure of enjoyment has an extra value *because* it is certain. No such assurance attaches to the purchase of a new car battery, or a new electric light bulb; though it looks just the same as all the ones that went before, and at first behaves the same, it may last a short time or a long one.

To a great extent, this uncertainty of future enjoyment is a nuisance. The man who insures against rain on his holiday is showing by his action that he regards the uncertainty of good weather as an evil which can be partly offset by a chance of financial compensation. It would be nice to be sure in advance that a toy will prove durable, or a gadget will actually work. However, the complex minds of human beings are capable of finding advantage as well as disadvantage in uncertainty. Some people enjoy gambling on future events. What are the circumstances in which they will wish to do so?

It is tempting to reply that some are born gamblers, and others are not. No one, however, would enjoy complete uncertainty in every aspect of their purchases; for instance, railways with no time-tables. We like to be surrounded by a little assurance of stability—prices not wholly arbitrary, repeat orders possible. No doubt some gamblers push their compulsive urge further into the detail of living than ordinary men, but generally speaking it seems likely that uncertainty is particularly attractive if it offers a chance of large (not trivial) and extra benefits: and if these benefits are supplementary to a basic standard of living, and do not involve (or are not thought to involve) a risk of destitution. (The gambler who risks his all seldom seems to believe that the risk is real.) Thus, the risk of rain on a holiday in Scotland is a nuisance, and not even phrasing it the other way round— a risk of dry weather—can make it attractive. But a holiday contract in which every hundredth visitor received an extra fortnight's holiday free of charge might well be attractive; it offers a benefit which is both large and apparently additional, even though the cost will in fact be paid by the other ninety-nine visitors.

This is not the place to explore attitudes to uncertainty in more detail; that has been well done elsewhere, notably in the elegant works of Professor G. L. S. Shackle. The relevant point, for the present purpose, is that uncertainty of benefit frequently but not always detracts from the enjoyment of a purchase of goods or services. Having stated this, I can summarize the relevance to the general argument of the book of the points brought out in this chapter. The flow of wealth to individuals, and the stock in their hands, consists of goods and services which may yield enjoyment in *prospect*, over a *period* (long or short) of use or consumption, and in *retrospect*. The enjoyment may be certain or uncertain; the uncertainty of enjoyment is generally a disadvantage, but on occasion uncertainty may be enjoyable in itself. Our pattern of spending may be distorted towards the ephemeral by the tendency to underestimate the prospect of enjoyment in retrospect—partly because that enjoyment is at uncertain occasions in the future, and partly because retrospective enjoyment, though frequently important, cannot usually be foreseen with certainty at the time of a purchase.

Note that there are really two kinds of uncertainty about future enjoyment. One attaches to the thing being enjoyed, which may not come up to expectations; the other relates to our circumstances at the time of the enjoyment. A bikini may be fully up to expectations in the soundness of its construction, but if it rains every day of a holiday, the owner may feel that it has yielded no enjoyment. A book bought for future reading may turn out, when opened, to belong to a class of literature of which the reader has in the meantime become tired. A garden may be planted to give enjoyment in old age, but the owner knows that he may die before it reaches an enjoyable maturity. A parcel of randomly mixed foreign stamps, in which the philatelist may chance to find one or two rarities, gives an example of pleasurable uncertainty attaching to the *product* being enjoyed. On the other hand, the bachelor of my acquaintance who solemnly bought a four-bedroomed house against the chance that he might marry and have children was, in a small way, getting pleasure from gambling on being married within a fairly short time.

This chapter has concentrated on the attitudes of consumers. Business men, buying factories or machines, are commonly assumed to take a more hard-headed attitude, deriving enjoyment solely from the actual operation of their equipment to make a profit, and not being much concerned with either the prospect or the retrospect of ownership. Similarly, public authorities may be supposed to have practical corporate minds, enjoying the ownership of (say) a public convenience while it is yielding its benefits to the public, but not being much interested in it before or after that period. It is, of course, conceded that business men enjoy the prospect of profit—and are willing to pay a price for a chance of profits at a future date—but this has no necessary relation to the enjoyment of the physical equipment which will help to produce the profit. However, both business men and those in charge of public spending are but human beings and ordinary consumers. Machines and buildings are quite capable of giving an enjoyment not directly related to their profitability or public use. This tends to give rise to an emotional desire to prolong their active life—a fact which may have some relation to the tendency of some parts of industry to keep old-fashioned equipment far too long. For instance, many people have an irrational attachment to railways—not just the dedicated amateur enthusiasts, but also some who direct railway operations. There is enjoyment to be derived, even from the antique minor details of the railway system, and consequently there is a tendency to retain them. Where they must be swept away, they may (like the Euston Arch) still yield enjoyment in retrospect. Thus some of what has been said about consumers carries over to other purchasers, but with the difference that the bias towards the ephemeral is less important, and there may be a tendency to prolong the use of machines and buildings for reasons related, not to profitability, but to the general enjoyment that use gives to their owners.

IV

ME (NOW) AND THEM (THEN)

In Chapter III I have drawn attention to the need to bring time into our consideration of the flow and stock of wealth. The interest there was in the possibility of savouring an enjoyment in anticipation and in retrospect, as well as at the time when it happens. But what happens if we are given a choice between an addition to our wealth next week or the same addition next year? It is generally assumed that we will prefer the nearer benefit, and this is expressed by saying that we "discount" the future, so that we hold as equal preferences a benefit next week and some *greater* benefit next year. It is not certain that this can be claimed as a universal law of human psychology; if you give a child a plate of cakes he will sometimes prefer to keep the nicest one till last, thus maximizing the pleasure of anticipation. But certainly there must be a frequent tendency to discount the future, for otherwise it would be difficult to explain the need in many societies to pay interest even on perfectly safe loans.

A person who prefers a benefit close in time may, over his lifetime, receive less real wealth than if he had waited for a larger future benefit. But we have to be careful not to say that he has stood in the way of his own satisfaction. At the relevant time at which to exercise his preference, he has found greater satisfaction in the immediate than in the deferred benefit. Consider, for instance, a money payment deferred to a distant time. As pointed out in the last chapter, different sorts of uncertainty may attach to such a benefit; we can distinguish four such sources of uncertainty. The *amount* of the payment may be uncertain: this is not necessarily a disadvantage, for the uncertainty may consist of the chance of getting no less then, but possibly much more, than what would be obtained at an earlier date. The *date* of the payment may be uncertain. The *real value* of the payment will almost always be uncertain—it is possible to guess fairly accurately what £100 will buy in a year's time, but not in ten years' time. Last, and most important, the *circumstances of the recipient* will be uncertain—or, if the benefit be very long delayed, be resolved only by the certainty of death. The pleasure of anticipation over long years is considerably reduced by the fact that one cannot accurately imagine one's situation at the end of the period.

There are thus excellent reasons for preferring nearby benefits. This, however, is the point of view of an individual making choices for his own lifetime, or a company or other corporate body choosing for the span of its future existence which its managers are able to imagine. It is true that in societies in which social status is strongly related to family origins and inherited wealth, the rich have been willing to look far ahead beyond their own lifetime, gaining present satisfaction from the thought of a benefit which assures the status of their children. But this has become relatively unusual in British society. Many people sacrifice present for future benefits to make a provision, often inadequate, for old age; but, once this provision has been made at some accepted level, it may well be that other decisions are made with a short horizon, that is to say a strong time-discount.

However, the satisfaction which a man obtains from his total economic environment is the product, not only of his own past decisions, but of many decisions of other people and bodies which have created that environment. In other words, his enjoyment of the stock or flow of wealth is affected by the surroundings in which the wealth is to be enjoyed—using "surroundings" in a broad sense, to cover (for instance) the institutional and social structure, as well as the physical actions of his neighbours. The possibility exists that individuals looking to their own enjoyment may jointly create unsatisfactory "surroundings" for themselves and their successors. And this is what does happen, as some examples will show.

I write these words in a house built in 1900. It is built to a standard of solidity and careful finish which is unknown today. The difference is in part the result of the change in the relative cost of building labour: many buildings of the past required an amount of workmanship which would today be exorbitantly expensive. Another reason is the levelling of incomes produced by taxation: a well-off man in 1900 could afford to spend a greater proportion of his income on housing than can his counterpart today, because less was taken in tax. But these are not wholly convincing reasons for the difference in standards, when one remembers that there has been a great increase in the real income of the country since 1900. The main reason is almost certainly the change in the time-span which the owner has in mind when ordering a house. In 1900, any substantial dwelling was expected to have a life of indefinite length, perhaps of many centuries. Now it is sometimes considered a virtue or advantage that a building should have a built-in obsolescence which will require its replacement after sixty or eighty years.

What appears to have happened[1] is that, because of economic pressures, those who order buildings have been forced to look more searchingly at the relation of costs to benefits, and have reacted by building what will last their own time. But in doing so they impoverish their own generation to some extent and future generations to a much greater degree. This generation is the poorer, not only because houses built to a low standard look shabby easily and are expensive to maintain, but because low standards eliminate the small things which give distinction to a building. Future generations will receive from our hands little of enduring beauty, and will have an immense problem of replacement—admittedly an opportunity for building to the latest standards, but expensive nevertheless.

Of course, there was poor quality speculative housing in the nineteenth century, and many medieval buildings, now famous, were badly built. But I doubt whether there has ever been a period in which the time-horizon

[1] See also page 113.

for building (of all kinds) has been so short, and in which so little has been created which is even capable, let alone worthy, of standing five hundred years. In travelling to other towns, I have often found myself thinking sadly that it is inconceivable that the equivalent of their best buildings could be constructed today. In much of the public sector, regulation ensures standards which are much below those tolerated in earlier generations. If one considers purely what we *can* do, the decline in standards is hard to justify, not only because the British community is much richer than it was in 1900 or earlier times, but also because the range of technical possibilities is now much wider. The economists are come amongst us, and we are organizing ourselves more effectively for immediate enjoyment, at the cost of the future.

The logical end to the search for immediate enjoyment, whatever the consequences, is to be seen in the (fixed) caravan, which supplies quite a high standard of house-room at a low price, at the cost of widespread disfigurement of areas which once were beautiful. The attitude that "it will last my time" affects the quality of our surroundings in other ways—for instance, in the workmanship of furniture.

In parts of the world, short-term and selfish attitudes lead to the exploitation of natural resources at a wasteful rate. This happens, for instance, with the repeated cropping of farms in dry areas, until the structure of the top-soil breaks down and it blows away. It happens with the over rapid exploitation of woods and forests, and the over-fishing of the seas. In some places, bad habits of husbandry have the excuse of poverty—the farmer or the fisherman is so near to starvation that he must get the best return this year, whatever happens in years that come after. But well-to-do farmers and wealthy companies are sometimes guilty of sacrificing the future to the present.

It may be that short-term and selfish views have a sociological explanation. In a stable society whose structure and technology change slowly, or not at all, the long-run consequences of selfish actions are known and assessed, and the pressure on the individual to remember the good of the community is strong. One thus gets accepted practices, for instance of leaving land fallow for a period in rotation, which protect the community from those who might exploit it for their own quick profit. The sense of history is strong, as may be noted in parts of Ireland, where men talk of Cromwell as though he died yesterday. The individual life is less significant, in relation to the continuity of the community. In contrast, the advanced urban society, with rapidly changing technology, is characterized by considerable mobility, so that many can escape from the pressures of a community simply by moving to another one. So much is changing so rapidly that there is no settled body of opinion on the effect of actions which are selfish and short-term, and no means by which the community can require attention to the general good, except slowly and imperfectly through legislation. Those who are clever at making a "quick buck", and then move on to exploit for their own benefit some other short-term situation, may (so long as they are successful) be folk heroes; while those who offer tiresome reminders of the long-run good of the community are regarded as obstacles in the way of progress. The conventional wisdom of economics stands ready to justify the pursuit of profit by the individual for his own lifetime, and those who propose other criteria of action can be condemned as interfering with the market process.

Something like this may explain why, though with increasing wealth it should be easier to take long views, in fact a shorter-term outlook predominates. But other social factors have their influence. The middle-class Victorian father needed to look forward, not only for his own lifetime, but also for those of his unmarried daughters, who might find it difficult to obtain independent employment. Now it is assumed that children at almost all levels of society will become financially independent—unless they suffer from mental or physical handicap, when there may be assistance available from the State. In an age of small business, wide fluctuations of trade, and frequent bankruptcies, the possession of accumulated or inherited wealth was an important insurance against disaster. A hundred years ago, if a man had no capital, only the Poor Law stood between him and starvation. Sickness was more important, too, and there was no State aid to protect against its unexpected costs. We find it difficult nowadays to recognize what a difference has been made to our attitudes by the lifting of the fear of death from the main years of working life.[1] The prudent man still insures, for he may have an accident, but (that apart) his fears of a sudden change in the economic position of his family will be slight. It was quite otherwise, when a sudden and uncontrollable epidemic might take the head of the family.

It is not surprising, therefore, that (for those able to save) the continuing good of their family was an important motive in the nineteenth century, and is less important today. The vestiges of the earlier attitude may perhaps be seen in landed families of long lineage, and in a few proud and substantial family firms. Here the aim is to defeat high taxation and death duties, and to retain the historic controlling interest of the family; and here you will find a man planting an avenue of trees which only his children will see to advantage, building solid structures for posterity, and conducting his business operations with an eye on advantages beyond his own lifetime.

But this is the exception. "I'm all right, Jack" is the slogan: look after "number one". The preference for nearby benefits goes all too easily with a preference for benefits which accrue to the person rather than the community. We thus have to erect a considerable apparatus of control, to ensure that the community's interest in the flow of wealth is not forgotten, but what we do is imperfect and inadequate. It is a depressing conclusion, for there is no obvious reason why, in the rich and advanced nations, the situation should get any better.

[1] See page 134.

V

A DIGRESSION ON PAPER WEALTH

IN the preceding chapters, I have been using the word "wealth" as the consequence of a flow of goods and services bought by the consumer, some of which (for example, houses and furniture) can form part of a stock of wealth. But when, in everyday speech, we talk of a "wealthy" man, we usually mean that he is *able* to buy a lot of goods and services because he has much "paper" wealth—such as entries in bank accounts, stock certificates in companies, and records of money lent at interest. Furthermore, it seems that this "paper" wealth can vary very greatly without any change to the real flow or stock of goods: as when one reads in the paper "Tens of millions of pounds were knocked off the value of securities on the Stock Exchange yesterday." It is therefore necessary to be clear about the relationship of paper wealth to tangible goods and the normal types of purchasable service.

If you have a million pounds in cash, or capable of being turned into cash, you can go out and buy a Rolls-Royce car whenever you like. This is an advantage. But is a million pounds desirable simply because it is equivalent, at one remove, to Rolls-Royces, luxury yachts, and private suites at Claridges? Experience suggests that this is not the whole truth. Rich men seem on occasion to like money for its own sake, without any clear plan to use it on tangible things, because it is the evidence of their own success, or because it accompanies a certain kind of power which they enjoy. If a society honours riches, either as evidence of a man's ability and public spirit, or of the degree of Divine favour shown to him, it is not surprising if the individuals in that society value riches, in part at least, as a means of climbing higher on the ladder of social approval.

Furthermore, a large bank balance and a good portfolio of marketable stocks and shares are not usually desired as a means of buying specified named things at precise future dates. Quite otherwise: they are desired because they provide, or can be made on demand to provide, the quality known as *liquidity*, which is the special feature of cash and of a current account balance in a reliable bank. The essential feature of liquidity is that it provides the opportunity, at a moment's notice, to concentrate purchasing power on a transaction, whether it is foreseen or unforeseen. It provides a mobile striking force of money, and thereby reduces the worry associated with the uncertainties of life and increases the fun obtainable from being able to satisfy the whim of the moment.

This is not to say that people never save money for specified purposes. Obviously they do, most notably in the form of provision for their old age. But this sort of saving or holding of wealth for a precise future purpose is a humdrum and unexciting act: the money is usually tied up securely until it is needed, that is to say the quality of liquidity is absent. Earmarked wealth of this kind cannot compare in psychological attractiveness with the holding of funds and securities which may never be needed, which may accumulate and multiply to an uncertain degree (the uncertainty being, in this case, generally the source of pleasant hopes rather than fears), and which at all times provide protection against adverse circumstances and the means to engage in special purposes.

These, then, are some of the advantages of "paper" wealth. But does it have any real existence, other than that derived from real goods and services? After all, the ordinary share certificate of a company appears to be simply a written means of proving part-ownership of the company—with all its factories and machines, stocks of materials and work in progress.

The truth is more complicated. Let us look first at that part of wealth which is already in fully liquid form, that is to say coins, paper money and bank balances on current accounts—which together I shall call simply "money". (To this we may add, as being "cash a few days away", balances on deposit accounts and holdings whose encashability is guaranteed by Government, for example in the Post Office Savings Bank or in various "small savings" media.) The essential point about all this money is that, once created, it has to be held by somebody—you can get rid of it only by transferring it, as a gift or as the consideration for a purchase, to someone else. Governments have power to create money, typically by authorizing the banks to satisfy the demands of more borrowers; for new bank loans are newly-created money. Various means of controlling and directing the money-creating activities of the banks and other lenders exist. It is also possible, especially in simple economies, for Governments to create money by printing notes, and using them to pay for the Government's purchases or for social benefits.

There is no doubt, then, that it is possible to create more money independently of any change in the ability of the country to produce real goods and services. If one April an eccentric Chancellor of the Exchequer was to send £1,000 in banknotes to every man, woman and child in the country, there is no doubt that to begin with we should all feel richer. But for how long? If every recipient of the £1,000 had an unsatisfied desire for liquidity, and simply kept the money in a box to provide a feeling of safety and wealth, without actually needing to use it, then nothing would have occurred to push up prices, and the sense of being richer would be justified. We can be sure, however, that some of the recipients would already have as much liquidity as they wanted, while others would come by chance to one of the occasions in life at which such extra money needs to be used. Thus there will be an additional demand for goods and services, not necessarily capable of being matched by an additional supply. There may be "too much money chasing too few goods", and prices will then rise, reducing the real value (for making purchases) of everyone's stock of money.

This conclusion is not quite inevitable: there are

circumstances, in which resources of all kinds are in need of employment, when a distribution of extra cash is a reasonable economic policy. But there is a presumption that, unless the economy is suffering from gross general unemployment, or its citizens have a great propensity to hoard money, the creation of a lot more money will tend to push up prices. It still does not follow that those who hold the money will feel on average no richer than before, for the rise in prices is not a precise mechanical effect; it may be large or small. Even if one could show that the value of money had fallen in exact proportion to its increased quantity, people would for a long time *feel* richer, for it is clear that most holders of "paper" wealth appreciate only slowly and imperfectly what rising prices are doing to the real value of their holdings. But there is no safe way here to political popularity, by making people feel richer even if in fact they are not; for there is a danger that the creation of a large quantity of money will so upset confidence as to encourage people to get rid of it as quickly as possible, leading to a runaway rise in prices and reducing everyone's stock of money to a negligible value.

To sum up this part of the argument then—it appears that there is a link between money holdings and the real flow of goods and services, so that the value of money adjusts itself to the real productivity of the country: but the link is an imperfect one, so that one certainly cannot say that wealth in the form of money is *merely* a token or symbol of real goods and services. But what about ordinary shares in companies? These, in their most familiar form, are evidence of an entitlement to a share in such profits as may be distributed by the directors. They also commonly (thought not always) give the shareholder a vote in electing the directors and in deciding certain key issues of policy, such as the extension of the firm's borrowing rights. But in the large companies, which in Britain and the United States control the greater part of economic activity, the voting rights of a shareholder are seldom of any use, because of the great difficulty of organizing an effective vote among numerous and scattered shareholders. The shareholders do not effectively control the company, except on rare occasions such as, for example, when they are asked to consider a take-over bid. We must therefore look to the distribution of profits to find the reason for holding wealth in this way.

The investor in ordinary shares (if they are readily marketable by being quoted on a stock exchange) generally has in mind *two* aspects of his ownership: one is the expectation of dividends over the period of his ownership, while the other is the expectation of capital profit, or the fear of capital loss, up to the date (known or unknown) when it may be convenient or necessary to sell his shares. There are some people, for example widows with a life interest in an estate, who are almost entirely interested in income rather than capital: and some who take pleasure in gambling, and pay a high rate of tax on income, whose eyes are fixed on capital gains—though the taxation of such gains has reduced their attraction as a sole reason for investing. Let us, however, consider a "normal" investor interested in both dividends and in changes in the value of his capital.

In both cases, what matters is not the ascertainable facts from the past, but the expectations for the future. Dividends depend in the long run on the profits of the company, and on the policy of the directors in distributing or retaining those profits. Thus there is implicit in the expectation of dividends a strong link with the real world—the growth, efficiency and competitiveness of the company, and the national factors and policies which bear on its success; but there is also an element which comes from the expectation of company policy, which may change with changes on the Board of Directors. The expectation of future capital values is even more complex. It contains two distinct elements—the hope of a quick gain in values, which might make it sensible to sell the shares to realize a part of the gains, and invest the proceeds elsewhere: and the expectation of value at some unknown future date when a change of circumstances might make it *necessary* to sell the shares. If the shares fluctuate widely in value, they may offer a hope of quick gain, but also a fear that, if that gain does not materialize and a forced sale becomes necessary, there might be a large loss. The expectations of capital value are only very distantly related to the capital value of the real assets of a company; if a company adds to its real assets but not to its profitability, the capital value of the shares is likely to be influenced by the profits gained rather than by the (apparently useless) additions to real assets.

Furthermore, expectations of future capital values are influenced by all sorts of guesses about the future course of the economy and the place of the company in it— for instance, its chances of being "taken over" at an attractive price. These expectations are consequently volatile, and it may become worth while for people to buy and sell the shares as a speculation, not because of any direct consideration about the operations of the company, but as a consequence of a guess about what other speculators are doing. When we add to this the fact that some companies are pure financial intermediaries, one or more removes of ownership away from the operating units which own factories and make products, it becomes very clear that paper wealth in the form of shares can offer both psychological satisfaction and real gain (or real loss) to an extent which is only partly and distantly related to the production of saleable things and the ownership of real assets.

The same applies, in an even clearer manner, to the ownership of securities issued by Government ("gilt-edged"). The income obtainable from these securities is normally fixed and known in advance, so that what matters is the *price paid for the right to that income* and the *expectation of future prices*. These are determined mainly by the terms of redemption of the security and by guesses about future Government policy and its effectiveness; if the rates which enter into the complex of rates of interest move upwards, the value of gilt-edged will fall, and vice versa. Government policy affecting rates of interest is not independent of the real world, but the relation is tortuous, involved and indirect, and may involve the internal affairs and institutional peculiarities of other countries. There is certainly no simple relation whatever between wealth in gilt-edged and the success of the nation; Britain maintained full employment and became substantially richer as a producing country in the twenty years after 1945, but a purchaser of undated British Government stock in that year has had both a miserably small income return, and a reduction of the capital value of his holding by more than half.

It is not necessary to discuss other forms of "paper" wealth in detail. The same conclusion will apply: that wealth in money and stocks and shares is not tied closely to the flow or stock of real goods, but can fluctuate for many reasons quite far distant from the productivity or real economic success of the country. These forms of wealth are important and psychologically attractive—part of the attraction being, not in the planned use of wealth, but in its continued holding as a reserve against unforeseen difficulties and opportunities. Because the connexion between the world of money and share certificates, and the world of factories which produce things and people who provide services, is so indirect and imperfect, it follows that the interests of the holders of paper wealth do not necessarily lie in the same direction as the interests of the nation as a producer of real things.

There are possibilities of harm which arise from this conflict. The nation is genuinely richer if it produces more goods and services which are needed, and makes them available to those who need them—or, of course, produces things which can be exchanged overseas for other things which are needed here at home. If there are unused productive resources, it will (from this point of view) be worth while to bring them into employment; this will generate more income, and, with the assistance of the tax and social security systems, new purchasing power can be brought into the hands of those who will want to buy the extra product. The simple-minded view that a nation cannot be better off by leaving those who can produce without employment is broadly correct. In Britain, however, an approach to full employment of labour gives rise to fears—of rising prices and wages, higher imports, declining exports, inability to pay our trading debts to other countries. Consequently we have repeatedly by our own volition, and recently under external pressure, depressed demand so as to create what is called, in the jargon, "a margin of unused capacity".

By this means we have lost many thousands of millions of pounds-worth of production. The loss is not only the direct consequence of producing fewer consumer goods; we also interfere with the growth of our capacity to produce more in future years. This is not the place to discuss the fundamental British economic problem. If it is assumed that only certain policies are appropriate (others, for instance direct import controls, being regarded by the conventional wisdom as impossible) the loss in production is largely inevitable. But the problem is made worse by the fact that some of the influences on policy come from those who are interested in "paper wealth" rather than "real wealth". They are interested, therefore, in maintaining the optimism of expectations, in creating "the right climate of opinion", and this may involve the execution of policies which are conventionally regarded as "safe" or "right" among those who hold money power.

This is the reality behind the myth of the "gnomes of Zurich". Britain's policies have had to conform to international financial opinion. Being in debt we have had no alternative. The economic views held among those who are mainly interested in money transactions are often mistaken or out of date—in particular, such people tend to have strong opinions, which eliminate certain possible policies as unthinkable. The financier lives in a world of the mind, where the most important factor is the reaction of other financiers. He deals in symbols, not real goods; but real goods may have to be sacrificed to maintain him in a state of confidence. The British devaluation of 1967, and the gold crises of 1968, illustrate both the great power of financial opinion, and its slight regard for the consequences for the production of real wealth. We pretend now that devaluation was an act of policy, but in fact it is seldom possible for a country to devalue of its own volition and at the right time; the change is brought about by external pressure, at a time which suits the country's rivals, not her friends. It is an economic defeat, and can in part be ascribed to the tenuousness of the links between the real world and that of paper wealth.

VI

KNOWING TOO MUCH

IT has long been observed that the degree of satisfaction produced by a certain flow or stock of wealth depends on what other people have got: so that satisfaction is, to some extent, a state of not having need to feel envy. Whereas at one time attempts were made to define poverty in absolute terms, a state of being unable to obtain minimum nutritional requirements and to have the bare essentials of house-room and clothing, the tendency in advanced countries now is to define poverty as a state of being well below the average. A poor man is one who manifestly cannot keep up with the Jones's, though fifty years ago he might have been counted well-off. (This relative definition is a godsend to propagandists, for it can be asserted as an incontrovertible fact that fifty per cent of the population have less than the median income.)

Let us analyse in greater detail the influence of our neighbours on our state of satisfaction. For this purpose our "neighbours" are those we regard as having a social position similar to, and in principle attainable by, ourselves. No strong feeling of envy is induced by hearing that a pop star has installed a gold-plated bath—except, perhaps, among other pop stars; to most of us, the life of such a star is an alien one, to be observed with interest from afar but having no contact with our own expectations. It follows that the more a society is divided into rigid social classes or castes, between which no significant mobility is expected, the narrower will we expect to find the range of income or wealth among a man's "neighbours", and consequently the less the dissatisfaction induced by observing the success of others. In a highly mobile society, there will be many people much richer than ourselves who came from the same origins; and the fact that we cannot buy as many things as they can is proof to the world of our own ineffectiveness.[1]

Of course, this conclusion is affected by the degree to which society honours things other than material success—either in general, or in particular groups of people. It is possible for a parson to go round in a coat frayed at the edges without an acute sense of dissatisfaction at his inability to be as tidy as a bank clerk; for there is still a sufficient residual belief that it is appropriate for a parson

[1] Samuel Smiles writes of the effects of "keeping up with the Jones's" in an eloquent passage of *Self-Help* (centenary edition, p. 290)—

"Middle-class people are apt to live up to their incomes, if not beyond them; affecting a degree of 'style' which is most unhealthy in its effects upon society at large. There is an ambition to bring up boys as gentlemen, or rather 'genteel' men ... and the result is, that we have a vast number of gingerbread young gentry thrown upon the world, who remind one of the abandoned hulls sometimes picked up at sea, with only a monkey on board."

"There is a dreadful ambition abroad for being 'genteel'. We keep up appearances, too often at the expense of honesty; and, though we may not be rich, yet we must seem to be so. We must be 'respectable', though only in the meanest sense—in mere vulgar outward show."

to live in holy poverty. (It is doubtful, however, if the same degree of insulation from the necessity to "keep up with the Jones's" will be readily felt by the parson's wife.) The dissatisfaction bred by the urge for social emulation is not confined to Western societies, nor to advanced countries. In a poor peasant society, the man with one cow will feel his poverty more acutely if his neighbour obtains two. But in societies with a very wide range of income, it is common to find social or institutional barriers which preserve the greater part of the population from any need to worry about the possibility of becoming rich. Envy of the unattainable is a less acute emotion.

The influence of our neighbours must clearly depend on the effectiveness with which we know about their standard of living, and they about ours. Both halves of this relationship are important. A hermit has, by definition, no neighbours to cause him to make comparisons. A dweller in a small community may only have a limited range of such comparisons to make: but he may also be conscious that everyone else knows exactly how he lives. In a village, inability to "keep up with the Jones's" can give rise to acute dissatisfaction, whereas in a great city, although there are apparently so many more Jones's to keep up with, the anonymity of existence is a protection: your neighbours may have little idea of how you live.

But knowledge not obtained directly can be simulated by the media of mass communication. This is a powerful influence indeed, but it is a selective one. It is aimed at the encouragement of extra purchasing by groups in the community which are large, homogeneous and wealthy enough to justify the cost of advertising. The greatest effect is exercised by advertising which can be repeated in a variety of forms in places widely seen, such as popular television programmes and the national Press. In British conditions, this tends to establish a norm of behaviour for the middle class rather than for the rich (who are too few) or the poor (who provide no adequate market); for women rather than men, since women are presumed to control a larger sector of purchases: and for the affluent and pliable young, rather than for those in later years of life who are set in their ways and have heavy commitments. Although there is of course a use of specialist media to affect the habits of special groups (such as cage-bird fanciers or landed proprietors), this is a matter of minor importance. To see the instrument of conformity working at its full power, by a combined use of editorial matter and advertisements, one must look at mass-circulation journals such as *Woman* and *Woman's Own*.

The effect of advertising, and of the conformist "image" provided by the editors of journals and television programmes as a setting for the advertisements, is thus to induce in younger women, of moderate means, a dissatisfaction which they might not have felt simply from observation of their neighbours. Whereas successive past generations, over long periods of time, enjoyed an average standard of living which altered only slowly, now the accepted norm must be raised every few years.

Poverty, which once was not having enough to eat, will before long mean the inability to instal a colour television set. The influence spreads outwards from those to whom it is primarily directed, from women to men and from younger to older people, but it weakens as it goes: note, for instance, the extreme difficulty of persuading any male over twenty-five to feel dissatisfaction with that insult to the aesthetic sense, the standard British dun-coloured raincoat. The influence stops short at those who, with their "neighbours", form an isolated group with its own standards. It is doubtful, for instance, whether the pages of *Woman* induce dissatisfaction among duchesses, nuns, or old ladies who live in country cottages.

But the complications of the effects of conformity with our neighbours and of advertising need to be pursued a little further. First, we must not assume that it is neces-sarily a bad thing that people should be induced to feel poorer than they had previously felt. The awakening of desires and the creation of dissatisfaction are important instruments of material progress. A peasant society can exist for generations, inefficiently scratching a bare living in largely self-sufficient communities. It is the itinerant salesman, the Scotch draper, who awakens the desire for new things produced in the towns or in other countries, and who thus creates the need to produce a surplus and earn some cash. The creation of dissatis-faction is an essential part of the transition to a market economy, which in turn is the prerequisite for large-scale and efficient production. In later times, the desire to copy one's better-off neighbours has had valuable results in improving sanitation, lessening disease, and freeing women from the necessity to work for long hours at household tasks. But, the higher the standard of living of a society, the more likely it is that "keeping up with the Jones's" or following the recommendations of the advertisers will yield little beyond the immediate psychological satisfaction. This is particularly true of the fashion industries in clothes, car-body styles, house decoration, and the like: by the time one has caught up with the Jones's, they have decided to do something different, so that the sense of relative poverty is perpetual.

For instance, a recent issue of *Woman* illustrates the conversion of an entrance hall so that it is decorated in gold, brown, orange and peacock blue. Against these vigorous colours stands the india-rubber plant, the fashionable modern equivalent of the aspidistra. The light shade is Japanese, shaped like a large orange. The style is what is known as "clean and uncluttered". Not long ago, however, this style would certainly have been interpreted in delicate pastel colours: a little later the device of papering one wall in a different paper would have been recommended: while the hall is illustrated, before redecoration, in the style of suburban respectability of the 1930s—leaded windows with stained-glass decorations, solid brown woodwork, shining linoleum floor: probably with a plain but durable and efficient flat white lampshade, or a lantern with coloured glass sides. The variations in taste thus implied, for a single small area, are both large and frequent. By next year, the Jones's may have moved on to pop-art wallpapers, illuminated by small chandeliers. There is little evidence that this cycle of change proceeds by successive approximation to higher levels of artistic achievement. Its main purpose is simply to *be* a change—which, while pleasant to the affluent consumer, is also profitable to manufacturers.

But one must not overestimate the efficiency of those who mould our attitudes. Hucksters calling their wares at times produce only a confused noise. The tremendous flood of propaganda, suddenly released two days after Christmas, to persuade us to book the next summer's holidays, produces no clear impression on the mind of what the Jones's are going to do—except, of course, buy one of several thousand packaged tours to the Continent. This is typical of the many cases in which competitive advertising achieves only a blurred and general image, rather than a clear urge to buy a particular thing. Nevertheless, this blurred image may be quite enough to induce dissatisfaction and a feeling of relative poverty: "everyone is going to the Continent this year (except me, and I'm only going to Brighton)". A more serious failure of attitude-moulding may occur if a large group of the population finds it particularly difficult to alter its way of living. Consider, for instance, an affluent council-house tenant, who already owns a television set, a washing machine, a refrigerator and a small car. He has no room for more kitchen equipment; there is little snob attraction in owning a larger car, unless one jumps to the luxury class: expenditure on central heating would not be incurred by a tenant. The house already has its full quota of furniture—the fat three-piece suite, the quilted bed-head, and so on. Where is the next major expenditure to be induced? Such a man has reached the top of a group within society, from which he cannot jump without making the large sacrifices necessary to buy a house of his own. If this change is impossible, much of the propaganda urging him to be dissatisfied and to raise his standard of living will pass him by.

If it were not for our need of social contacts, we would certainly feel happier and wealthier if we could live like hermits, without comparing our standard of living with that of others, and with the assurance that others are not looking critically at our own way of life. The various methods of influencing our attitudes, both direct advertising and the more subtle consensus of opinion in the organs of communication (for example that "mini-skirts are *in* this year"), further increase our dissatisfaction, with results which, though sometimes to the public advantage, become less so as the standard of living rises. In this sense, "knowing too much" is a subtraction from the real advantages of a stock or a flow of wealth.

Thus far I have concerned myself with attitudes, but there are also real effects of the artificially induced flow of knowledge which are unfavourable. In order to persuade us to buy, unnecessary and non-functional changes are made in products (thus making last year's model look out of date), and durability is often sacrificed to obtain a quick sale based on price and eye-appeal.

(I have never yet, for instance, seen an electric iron which is really well constructed and can give reliable service over many years.) Though much poorer than ourselves, our ancestors of a century ago are often said to have got "better value for money"—not just from cheaper prices, but from buying articles sturdily made to perform their function over a long time. In Chapter III I have pointed out that some goods at least will certainly be cast aside before they are worn out; it would be wasteful to make them everlasting. But, if the flow of goods being produced contains an increasing proportion of articles designed with too short a life, with excessive "built-in obsolescence",[1] without offering the consumer the alternative of longer-lasting articles at a comparable price, the change in the money measure of wealth may become unreliable as a measure of satisfaction actually achieved. The problem here is not that we know too much, but that the knowledge forced upon us by skilful propaganda is of irrelevant things. The cloth looks beautiful in the colour pages of the fashion magazines, but no one reminds us that it will shrink and the colour will wash out.

It is worth reminding ourselves, however, that we hardly ever spend our money with complete knowledge of all the choices available on the market, and of their qualities of construction or design. Our satisfactions and dissatisfactions, our feelings of wealth or poverty, are related to the particular selection of information built up from past and present observation, from the talk of our

[1] See page 115.

neighbours, and from the media of communication. What the advertisers are doing is to alter this imperfect selection of information so as to increase dissatisfaction, in the hope that we shall find relief in buying their product.

VII

TOO MANY STATISTICS

THE title of this chapter will be greeted with no enthusiasm by my economist friends. How can we possibly have too many of those valuable little numbers which offer us a hope of finding an accurate guide to public and private policy? With the sad passing of *Bradshaw's Railway Guide*, the reference to the use of British official statistics in the formation of public policy as being like "looking up the trains in last year's Bradshaw" has an archaic sound; but it is still true that there are many areas in which our statistical knowledge is imperfect, erroneous, incomplete or grievously slow, and our policies therefore depend on guesswork.

But I return to the point made at the end of the last chapter. Perfect information is not an attainable ideal, except in trivial affairs. An excess of facts, even if they are completely accurate and up to date, can be as inhibiting to decisions as a deficiency. Clarity of understanding does not grow indefinitely with a growth of information, for eventually the mind is submerged and confused by the flood of facts and impressions. We operate, necessarily and at all times, in all important decisions of life, on information which is incomplete and imperfect. The proper exercise of our skill is not to create an unmanageable flow of information, but to select what is important, relevant and timely.

What is the relevance of this to our appreciation of the stock or flow of wealth? Day by day, those who live in "advanced" countries receive from newspapers, radio and television, from politicians, expert commentators, and some not so expert, a great flood of information relevant to our appreciation of individual or national wealth. We learn of the increases in other people's incomes and of the way they live. We have laid before us international comparisons, and in particular those which tell us of our position in various "league tables" of income, or of the rate of growth of income. In Britain especially, we are told many things which are relevant to the uncertainties and dangers of our economic position: the rise and fall of gold and convertible currency reserves, the fluctuations of the exchanges within their permitted limits, the deficit on visible trade, the views of foreigners about the appropriateness of our economic policies. From all the information coming forward, we select some for attention (for we cannot absorb it all); but we are in no position to select a truly balanced set of facts.

Thus, at the individual level, the facts which reach us are of wage and salary demands and wage increases, and of the many things which (so the advertisers tell us) people just like ourselves are able to buy. Extreme poverty is still newsworthy, but most people do not regard themselves as likely to fall into such poverty, and what we hear and see does not therefore induce the same thankfulness for good fortune: "there, but for the grace of

God, go I". The broad effect of the information crowding in on us is to induce envy and dissatisfaction, and to lessen our enjoyment of a given stock or flow of wealth. A peasant in an isolated village judges his wealth by what he himself has known, either in his past life or in a limited circle of neighbours: but the educated worker in the industry or commerce of an advanced country is open to influences both more widespread and more random.

The effect at the national level is, in Britain at least, more dangerous. Throughout the recent years of the country's economic difficulties, the product or flow of wealth produced by the nation, and the average standard of living of its people, have continued to rise. The words for which Mr. Macmillan was so often attacked, "You've never had it so good", have been literal statistical truth, for the great majority of the population. But rising prosperity has been associated with an increasing sense of economic failure and of national poverty. The chief evidence of this failure lies in the balance of overseas payments, but the deficit here is generally small in relation to the nation's production and indeed in relation to its own possible statistical error. (The deficit shown in the monthly trade accounts signifies little by itself, for Britain by long experience must normally expect to have a deficit in its visible trade, offset by "invisible" surpluses.) The fluctuations of gold and convertible currency reserves relate to only a part of our overseas assets and liabilities. The comparisons which show the relative slowness of British economic growth are reasonably well founded, but they record a difference which has existed for a long time, and it is not self-evident that this is a league in which we should want to be champions. The real cause for concern is not that a Britain, already quite well off, is failing to achieve rapid growth, but that many countries which are much worse off are falling even further behind us.

In the days before economic and statistical information was well developed, crises blew up like storms, showing themselves in business failures, runs on the banks, and losses of gold. When the weather experts give us advance warning of a storm, we can take action to protect ourselves, but we cannot (so far) influence the storm itself. But advance warning of economic storms enables people, not only to take shelter, but by their actions to change the course of economic events. The change is not necessarily for the better: and the satisfaction or welfare of those involved in the events is not necessarily improved by their foreknowledge. Although in theory speculators, looking forward and taking action in their own interests, might moderate the fluctuations of the economy, in practice the mass dissemination of economic facts tends to produce, not a balanced understanding, but exaggerated moods of pessimism or optimism. The troubles with the British balance of payments provide a striking example of this; they have unquestionably been made worse by exaggeration and pessimism induced by the constant flow of information.

Our state, indeed, is much like that of a patient, who fears that he has a serious disease, and is told his temperature and blood pressure every hour. This parallel is not a fanciful one. Expectations are a powerful influence on economic events, and on the satisfaction we receive from economic goods. The state of mind of the actors in the economic system is a matter of great importance, and the ills of the system can be "psychosomatic" just like diseases of the body.

This is no argument against good information, wisely interpreted. We do not want our economic doctors to keep the truth from the patient. But, as we are learning, now that computers have so greatly increased our statistical potential, there is more to information than piling it up. Twenty years ago in Britain (and perhaps thirty years earlier in the US) we were so short of statistical information that any addition was something to be thankful for. Though there is still much to find out, it is time that we asked ourselves whether in some areas less volume or frequency of publication, with more interpretation, might not serve our needs better.

I doubt, for instance, whether the frequent publication of the total of gold and convertible currency reserves—a figure both partial, and capable of being "window-dressed"—does any good. Quarterly trade accounts would be quite adequate, for even the most skilled observers find it difficult to interpret the monthly fluctuations. I question if even the monthly index of industrial production is much use, as a means of assessing rates of growth or observing turning-points, for the preliminary figures are often revised and the month-to-month changes may thus be misleading. In fact, I suggest that the general principle should be to reduce all statistical information about the economy to quarterly publication (at most), unless a clear case can be made that more frequent figures will have some meaning and will be used. The marginal unit of statistical resources would be much better used in improving the quality of data and speeding their presentation after the end of the period to which they relate, rather than in more frequent publication. Furthermore, it is not worth while publishing a mass of short-term information when the facts about the broad structure of the economy are so out of date. (This particularly affects index numbers, whose "weights" may be derived from periodic censuses.) Useful information for the management of the economy and of businesses could be obtained from the Census of Production, but this is now so slow as to be almost useless; and the Census of Population, in its detailed tabulations at least, has been little better.

Perhaps the most important reform in the statistical system, however, would be to publish far more informed commentaries on the figures (including comments on their accuracy, where this seems called for). This would check the tendency to make irrelevant statistical comparisons, and to use statistics as a way of stimulating a psychosomatic illness of the economy. Both our enjoyment of the wealth we now possess, and our ability to create more, are harmed by the indiscriminate use of statistics. Before the computers turn the flow into a flood, we should think again.

VIII

WEALTH AND INDIVIDUAL HAPPINESS

I BEGIN this stage of our inquiry by asking why people want to be paid more. As throughout this book, my concern is with the advanced countries; obviously a large proportion of mankind want more because they have less than a minimum reasonable provision of food, clothing and shelter. This is true also of some, even in the richest countries, but such under-privileged people are often ill-organized, and receive help gradually either from charity or as a consequence of increases received by others. I concentrate attention, therefore, on those who plainly already have more than a minimum of food, clothing and shelter.

It is well established that most people think they are worth somewhat more than they are now receiving; that is, that they think they ought to be a rung higher on the ladder. But what determines what they actually get? There is no simple answer in terms of the demand for and supply of labour. An employer will not, in normal cases, knowingly continue to employ a worker who produces a value less than his wage. This, however, tells us that, *given* the wage, the employer will adjust the number of workers he employs until the last and least efficient one is producing only just a little more than his wage. It would still be possible for the wage to be fixed by some external compulsion—for instance, by Government edict.

There is, of course, a broad influence of demand and supply within occupations. People are trained for particular occupations, and do not find it easy to cross the borders into others. If, therefore, the demand for labour in a particular occupation falls (as the consequence, for instance, of technical change or of the decline of an industry) there is a presumption that wages will go up more slowly or even fall. If the supply of labour dries up (for instance, because the occupation is dangerous or unfashionable) there is a presumption that wages may rise more than the average amount. But these are very broad, long-run, general presumptions, and plenty of exceptions can be found. For instance, the newspaper printing industry has for long shown a combination of excess labour (in relation to the technological requirements) and very high wages.

Examples like this lead people to treat the determination of wages and salaries as a straight case of the balance of power between organized labour and organized employers. There are two extremes: one, a wage so high that the employer would go out of business (or dispense with the use of the relevant grade of labour) rather than pay it: the other, a wage so low that the worker would strike for an indefinite period, or leave the industry, rather than tolerate it. Between these two extremes (it is argued) the solution depends on the relative strength of the two sides. This theory will not of course do for the considerable number of people whose pay is not fixed by bargaining but by the straight offer of a rate by the employer—for instance, domestic help, and much office staff. But even in a simple trade union bargaining situation, many questions are left unanswered about the way in which a final solution is reached, particularly where the "open warfare" of strikes and lockouts is not reached.

To make progress, we must look at some sociological facts. One is that the two sides in negotiations share certain assumptions about what is "just" and "reasonable". These assumptions no doubt vary from one country to another. In Britain it is very generally assumed, first that workers (up to quite a high rate of pay) ought to be compensated for changes in the cost of living, and second that workers ought at least to share in the fruit of rising productivity, even if this is quite unrelated to any change in their own effort. The first of these assumptions can be phrased more accurately, namely, that gross wages (before tax and insurance deductions) should vary with the cost of living; this leaves open a possibility that the Government can force a reduction in the standard of living by higher taxation, though the union side will on occasion try to extend the argument to *net* wages, thus (if they are successful) protecting their members from any reduction whatever in their standard of living. The second assumption will still leave open an area for bargaining—unions often demand, not only the whole of a realized gain from higher productivity, but advance payment in respect of a gain not yet realized. The important point, however, is that employers do not argue strongly against *some* compensation for this reason.

The prevalence of these agreed assumptions goes far to account for the persistence of inflation in Britain, and for the difficulty in obtaining price reductions which might win new export markets. But their power is greatly increased by another assumption widely shared by the parties to negotiations, namely that "customary relationships and differentials should be maintained"; that is, that a wage change in another occupation (influenced perhaps by quite different conditions of demand, supply and productivity) is a strong argument for a similar change in the occupation to which the negotiations relate. This system can be seen in a pure state in the Irish Republic, which has periodic "rounds" of wage adjustment, in which a change in one occupation is rapidly generalized over many others. Of course, economic forces do gradually alter customary differentials, but the resistance to alteration is strong, and the linking of rates in this way means that increases which are justified (for example to attract more entrants) are passed on to occupations where no justification exists.

The argument from customary differentials is sometimes pushed to ridiculous extremes. I have heard argument for an increase in wages in a small and dying trade (which, if it paid the increase, would certainly die much quicker) related only to the maintenance of parity with another trade producing, from the same raw material, a totally unrelated product. One trade served a specialized industrial use, the other a women's fashion trade; the latter had secured an increase simply because of a change in fashion. The significant point was that the employers in the dying trade, though they stood in danger of bankruptcy, did not dispute the power of the argument that a relationship which could be traced back half a century should continue indefinitely.

We have here a clue to the nature of people's attitudes to pay. Those of an age to work acquire status in the eyes of the community, either from their work or (if a woman) from being married to someone with that status. This is why unemployment would be damaging, and regarded as intolerable, even if it brought no financial hardship; those who think that raising the dole would make unemployment acceptable are not facing the facts. It is degrading (in the exact sense of that word) to have no work. Even the family connexions of royalty go up in public esteem if they can be seen to be holding down a job.

Work confers status; but the exact status it confers is given by a social classification of jobs, which is seldom explicitly discussed, but is absorbed imperceptibly through everyday conversation. Most workers, in consequence, have a clear idea of their status in relation to some "neighbouring" jobs, and a rougher idea of a longer status list. The list is not rigidly arranged according to pay—for instance, the status of a parson or minister is considerably higher than his income would justify—but changes in pay are quickly understood to be an interference with the order of the list. It must not be thought that the preoccupation with "differentials" is confined to lower-paid workers. I have heard university professors explain, first that they consider their pay to be adequate, but second that they greatly resent an increase just given to higher civil servants, and consider that the same increase should speedily be given to all university staff. In fact, the higher up the pay scale one goes, the more likely it is that the interest in money will be as a guarantee of status, rather than because of the urgency of the need to spend it.

Many professional and white-collar workers are on pay scales which give annual increments over a long stretch of their early working life—and also, of course, increases when the whole scale is changed, every two or three years. In contrast, many operatives (over the age of twenty-one) are on fixed time rates, or on piece rates, without relation to age; but those workers often expect an adjustment of wage scales almost every year. There is no clear justification for this different relationship to age; it has grown up, but is now the subject of a firm social distinction, which corresponds broadly (though not exactly) to the difference between "salaries" and "wages".

George Bernard Shaw wanted equality of pay, provided everyone was levelled up to his (considerable) income. But the social differences embodied in pay differentials are strongly resistant to change. The end of Marco and Giuseppe's campaign for equality—

> The Chancellor in his peruke—
> The Earl, the Marquis, and the Dook,
> The Groom, the Butler, and the Cook—
> They all shall equal be.

> The Aristocrat who banks with Coutts—
> The Aristocrat who hunts and shoots—
> The Aristocrat who cleans our boots—
>   They all shall equal be!

was the cautionary tale from Don Alhambra of the King who

> . . . wished all men as rich as he
> (And he was rich as rich could be),
> So to the top of every tree
>   Promoted everybody.
>   .   .   .
> That King, although no one denies
> His heart was of abnormal size,
> Yet he'd have acted otherwise
>   If he had been acuter.
> The end is easily foretold,
> When every blessed thing you hold
> Is made of silver, or of gold,
>   You long for simple pewter.
>   .   .   .
> In short, whoever you may be,
> To this conclusion you'll agree,
> When every one is somebodee,
>   Then no one's anybody!

The really puzzling thing about pay differentials is not their existence, but what governs their size. A professor in a university earns about three and a half times as much as an assistant lecturer: but why three and a half? Why not any other number greater than one? If, by sudden decree, we could divide all existing differentials by ten, bringing everyone much nearer to the average rate of pay, would satisfaction be greatly reduced? Skilled men would still earn more than unskilled, and managers more than the men they manage. Does the present structure have a reason, or is it just an historical accident?

There is no clear answer to this, but plainly it would be difficult to reduce differentials suddenly, because the present rates of the higher incomes yield a standard of living which has become customary and whose disappearance would be resented. For our present purpose, the point to be made is that the enjoyment or happiness yielded by a particular income is compounded of the satisfaction caused by the standard of living it gives, and the satisfaction caused by the status which it represents and guarantees. The desire for more wealth is strongly influenced by the desire for higher status—indeed, in some instances, this may be the only operative motive.

It follows from Chapter III that the pleasure which income provides can be an enjoyable expectation or retrospect, as well as an enjoyment at the time of consumption: and from Chapter V that the possession of a reserve of money ("liquidity") which can be switched at will to meet the unexpected need gives satisfaction. Consequently the expectation that income will show a surplus over essential needs, and will thus give rise to a reserve, is a source of pleasure, as Mr. Micawber knew—

Annual income twenty pounds, annual expenditure nineteen nineteen six, result happiness. Annual income twenty pounds, annual expenditure twenty pounds ought and six, result misery. The blossom is blighted, the leaf is withered, the God of day goes down upon the dreary scene, and—in short you are for ever floored.

It follows that part of the satisfaction to be derived from income is related to the degree of assurance about its future amount. An absolute guarantee that next year's income will be bigger than this year's, by an amount which exceeds the expected rise in prices, is obviously a source of enjoyment in anticipation. Thus a member of a university staff may find himself, at the age of about twenty-eight, holding an appointment to age sixty-seven, terminable only if he falls into some grave delinquency, and with annual increments in the early years of five to seven per cent. This happy state may be contrasted to that of (say) an actor or freelance journalist, who may be quite uncertain of any income next year whatever, apart from the minimum provided by Social Security benefits. But an assurance about next year's income, which is not related to an amount which will yield a surplus, is far less satisfactory. Many wage-earners are reasonably secure, but their future income is fully committed for basic living expenses and hire-purchase payments, so that they cannot look forward to the appearance of any free reserve to be used in new and pleasant ways.

Chapter VI is a reminder that our enjoyment of a given income is influenced, both by the actions of our neighbours, and by the flow of information and propaganda which reaches us, notably from advertisers. We can now link this to what has been said above about the status conferred by income. This status can exist and be recognized, even if the person who holds it is unorthodox in his habits of expenditure, but there is no doubt that one of the main ways of proclaiming status to the world is to adopt the habits of living of "the Jones's" of similar standing. The business man who said "My men expect me to run a Bentley; they would feel that a Jaguar was not quite good enough" was probably transferring to others his own belief about the right car to choose as a symbol of his status. It is easy to think of many examples of habits of living which proclaim status: the drinking of wine instead of beer: enthusiasm for a menu of smoked salmon, scampi, steak and Coupe Jacques: membership of appropriate clubs: real instead of simulated furs for the wife: private education for the children: employment of an *au pair* girl, or (at a higher level) of a resident man-servant: a full range of kitchen appliances, including whichever one is only just coming in (currently a waste grinder). It is probably those who are most insecure and unsure that they deserve a status who take most pleasure in exhibiting these external symbols.

If the desire for status is strong, it follows that the happiness induced by a certain level of income is a function, not of the absolute level of that income, but of its relation to the expenditure necessary to maintain the appropriate status. This is a most important point. The state which we describe as "shabby genteel" is one in which an income is overstretched in the attempt to maintain the outward appearances of status.[1] It is likely to be one of low satisfaction, even though the income may not be low in absolute terms. On the other hand,

---

[1] See page 63, footnote 1.

a small business man or farmer who is doing rather well may feel under no compulsion to claim (by the nature of his purchases) a higher status, so he may have the satisfaction of a surplus which he can either accumulate or switch to any goods he may desire.

For most people, habits of expenditure adjust themselves to rising income, though with a time-lag. There is thus a tendency to create the conditions for claiming a higher status; and, if the claim is in fact made, the income-receiver becomes vulnerable to any reduction of income, for there is a "ratchet effect"—it is much easier to tolerate moving up the social scale than down. The extreme case is one in which a person's idea of status adjusts itself quickly with each income rise, so that the desired status-expenditure is always running ahead of income. This was the sad state of the old woman who lived in a vinegar bottle; it means that satisfaction is never increased with rising income. Many people observe in themselves a milder version of the same attitude, and complain that, despite rises in (real) income, they "don't know where the money goes", and they "never seem to be any better off".

It may seem that a failure of satisfaction to increase with income is inconsistent with the normal presentation by economists of the theory of demand, which supposes that consumers get more "utility" or attain "preferred" points as their incomes climb. The inconsistency is in part explained by an abstraction from the adjustment of status expectations over time: tastes are assumed constant, and the whole pattern of utility (or indifference map) would change if a change in tastes were admitted. But the more careful economists (see page 26) have not claimed to be measuring anything to do with satisfaction, but simply observing in the actions of purchasers the strength of their *desire*—

> Wealth must possess utility. Utility, however, measures the strength of our desire for a commodity—its "*desiredness*" —not its desirability.[1]

The development of Marshall's phraseology on the subject illustrates the difficulty of expressing the point in a satisfactory way. In what was, in the eighth edition of the *Principles*, Book III, Chapter III, he had in the first edition related utility to "happiness" and "benefit". In the second edition he describes it as the "pleasure giving" or "pleasure affording" power. In the third edition it is the "benefit giving power", yielding "satisfaction". In the fourth edition he speaks of the "total pleasure or other benefit". By the fifth and later editions, influenced by an article by Pigou (*Economic Journal*, March 1903), he points out that *neither* desire *nor* satisfaction can be measured directly, but is content to make "the measure-ment which economics supplies . . . serve, with all its faults, *both* for the desires which prompt activities and for the satisfactions which result from them". In a letter to Pigou in 1903 he tries to distinguish satisfaction "that arises out of the number and excellence of the things which a man has" from that arising "out of the quality of the man himself". This, I suppose, implies that a

[1] SIR ALEXANDER CAIRNCROSS, *Introduction to Economics*, Chapter 2.

Cheshire cat has an innate happiness, which is the floor on which saucers of milk and other good things pile up further increments of happiness. The point is no doubt valid: all our discussion of income as yielding individual happiness, satisfaction, pleasure or benefit must be taken to refer to *increments* of these shadowy quantities.[1]

Thus far, then, we note that the happiness associated with a given income depends on the status to which the person aspires, and on the intensity of his or her interest in status. It does not follow, however, that a person who is content to remain in the same "station in life", and who obtains a rising real income, will *necessarily* in consequence attain higher levels of enjoyment. For the level of expenditure considered appropriate to the status may change, and, as we have seen in Chapter VI, a considerable industry of advertising and propaganda exists to cause it to change. This raises new issues, to which I revert below.

Two more points should be mentioned first, one obvious and frequently made, the other somewhat neglected. The first point is that both satisfaction and dissatisfaction can arise from both work and leisure—

[1] Marshall is not, of course, to be caught ignoring the problem of status-symbols. "In England now a well-to-do labourer is expected to appear on Sunday in a black coat, and, in some places, in a silk hat; though these would have subjected him to ridicule but a short time ago. There is a constant increase both in that variety and expensiveness which custom requires as a minimum, and that which it tolerates as a maximum; and the efforts to obtain distinction by dress are extending themselves throughout the lower grades of English society." (*Principles of Economics*, **III**, II, 2).

work can be interesting (and productive of status) or fatiguing, leisure can be full and creative or boring—but income is likely to be higher, the more work a man does and the less leisure he has. Three general statements can be made about the relation of income to leisure in Britain—

(*a*) Some workers can exchange leisure for income by working overtime.

(*b*) Those with fixed hours of work can in some instances supplement their income by taking spare-time jobs, and reducing their leisure time.

(*c*) Those with high incomes tend nowadays to work longer hours than those with low incomes.

The net state of satisfaction which a man reaches is therefore a complicated function of—

(i) The net satisfaction of his work: and this may fall as he does more hours of work, because of fatigue.

(ii) The net satisfaction of his leisure: and this may fall as he has more hours of leisure, because boredom becomes dominant.[1]

(iii) The satisfaction yielded by his income, which may depend on his choice of hours of work.

(iv) The opportunity which he has to spend and enjoy his income, which falls as he does more work. As a consequence of (*c*), those with high incomes often have the least leisure to enjoy them.

[1] As Keynes remarked, "To those who sweat for their daily bread leisure is a longed-for sweet—until they get it". He went on to quote the charwoman's epitaph—

"Don't mourn for me, friends, don't weep for me never,
For I'm going to do nothing for ever and ever."

We can imagine a man first balancing his work-time against his leisure-time, and then considering whether, if he works more, the extra income will outweigh the disadvantages of extra fatigue at work and diminished leisure. But too much extra income will take so much from leisure time that there will be no opportunity to enjoy it. If he fails to get the final balance right, people will say "What is the use of earning so much when you can't enjoy it?" or, "What is the use of having time off if you've got no money to spend?"

The point which is often neglected is the disadvantage of the sheer hard work of managing and spending a large income.[1] This is of course a minority effect, though writers in the United States often refer to the burden of managing numerous machines and gadgets, which often go wrong and are hard to service. If the housewife can have a "spending spree" once a year, this is an enjoyable if tiring occasion; but the woman who lives in a large house, requiring frequent purchases and orders for repairs, may well go beyond the point at which shopping and the use of money are enjoyable, while her husband will be oppressed by the keeping of accounts for tax purposes, the arrangement of insurances or mortgages, and much other financial business.

The very rich sometimes delegate the management of their incomes to professionals and assistants, but at an intermediate level people are occasionally heard to wish they could return to the comparative simplicity of relative poverty.

[1] See page 119.

When Keynes wrote his *Essays in Persuasion* he distinguished between the needs of human beings which are "absolute" and "those which are relative only in that their satisfaction lifts us above, makes us feel superior to, our fellows. Needs of the second class, those which satisfy the desire for superiority, may indeed be insatiable; for the higher the general level, the higher still are they. But this is not so true of the absolute needs—a point may soon be reached ... when these needs are satisfied in the sense that we prefer to devote our further energies to non-economic purposes". The absolute needs provide the "economic problem" of obtaining adequate satisfaction from scarce resources, and of this he wrote—

> ... assuming no important wars and no important increase in population the *economic problem* may be solved, or at least within sight of solution, within a hundred years. This means that the economic problem is not—if we look into the future—*the permanent problem of the human race.*[1]

In this forecast Keynes was probably wrong, for the reason that an "important increase in population" is taking place and seems likely to continue. Those of us who live in advanced countries may indeed be enjoying a particularly fortunate era of human existence; our great-grandchildren, despite all the advantages of high technology, may find it difficult to live as well in an overcrowded world depleted of many important natural resources. But in the meantime, as Professor J. K. Gal-

---

[1] op. cit. pp. 365–6.

braith pointed out with such vigour in *The Affluent Society*, the richest countries have carried forward from an age of poverty an urge to produce, when within their own boundaries the need for more production is no longer so urgent—the "absolute" need, in Keynes's sense, having largely disappeared.

The reason for giving so much attention to production is again in part a social one. Men obtain status by the fact of being producers; to be unemployed is to be rejected by society as a thing of no service. Unemployment benefit is no answer, for people have no desire to be paid to live in idleness. The greatest of all economic imperatives is the provision of full employment—by which is meant the sharing of the work of the community among all those who by social convention belong to the labour force, even though it might be possible to produce more by sacking stupid, inefficient or handicapped workers, and concentrating on those who are fully efficient. With this desire for the spreading of work, however, goes an ambiguous attitude towards the reduction of hours of work. It may well be inefficient (in a particular occupation) to work more than fifty or fifty-five hours a week, for the effect of fatigue may outweigh the production in the extra hours. At forty-five hours, extra effort and attention may keep production as high as it was at fifty, but at twenty hours, production per worker would obviously be likely to be much less. There is thus a rather ill-defined zone of high production. In practice, the actual hours of work decline rather slowly, and tend to remain in or about the zone of high production. Of course, the reduction of the standard working week is often an object of trade union bargaining, but this, when obtained, is often accompanied by an increase in overtime worked; or, if hours are cut sharply, one sees an increase in interest in taking additional part-time jobs.

All this does not fit in very well with the idea of work as laborious and unpleasant, and leisure as almost always preferable. In fact, apart from those who (like myself) enjoy our work and can hardly have too much of it, a much larger number find even laborious, dull, or repetitive work at least as pleasant as the uses to which they would put an increase in leisure. Apart from giving a man a place in the world, work offers him entry to a social grouping outside his home and family. The vision of a world so technologically efficient that all we need can be produced in twenty or ten hours is not really at all attractive, and is not made so by talking about the "constructive use of leisure". Some people—say, creative artists, and those with an urge to work voluntarily for social improvement—can do with all the leisure they can get. But there is really no evidence that, with fuller education, everyone will find set free within him potentialities which he can realize in long new stretches of leisure time. Far too many of us will remain like the child who, on a wet afternoon, drives his mother to distraction by wailing "Mummy, what shall I do *next*?"

The combination of the belief that everyone (except children at school, the elderly, and some of the housewives) should share in paid work, with the unwillingness to tolerate excessive leisure and with the growth of productivity relentlessly caused by technological change, results in an ever swelling flood of goods and services. In Britain, as in the United States, it is still possible to welcome this because there are so many public, communal jobs to be done. Old houses need to be rebuilt, transport to be modernized, education to be improved, health services to be made more effective. But in Britain, as in the United States, there is resistance to doing enough of these things. In the short run, in Britain, this can be ascribed to the need to export more, but behind this stands the general unwillingness to be taxed to pay for communal functions. No slogan is so popular as a promise to reduce Government expenditure.

We thus have the ridiculous situation that in Britain, a moderately affluent country, efforts must be made to whip up and maintain a consumer demand for quite unnecessary things, while many urgent communal purposes go unserved. The United States is on the same road, but further along it. There thinkers treat with serious concern the problem of how to maintain demand at a level high enough to use the products of the economy. Even when a large part of that product is being used for military purposes, there remains a great deal of non-essential expenditure which requires constant stimulation. That uncomfortably realistic satirical work, *Report from Iron Mountain*, considers what might be done if war were no more—

> If modern industrial societies can be defined as those which have developed the capacity to produce more than is required for their economic survival . . . military spending

can be said to furnish the only balance wheel with sufficient inertia to stabilize the advance of their economies. The fact that war is "wasteful" is what enables it to serve this function.

The writer goes on to argue that an economic surrogate for war must be correspondingly wasteful. He sees difficulty in large social welfare programmes, but points out the advantages of giant space-research programmes—

> What has been implied, though not yet expressly put forth, is the development of a long-range sequence of space-research projects with largely unattainable goals ... Space research can be viewed as the nearest modern equivalent yet devised to the pyramid-building, and similar ritualistic enterprises, of ancient societies.

Generally, however, hope is considered to lie in the unending stimulation of wasteful expenditure of a more domestic kind: that is, the purchase of more and more elaborate inessentials by ordinary consumers. Instead of production taking place to satisfy wants, wants are created to justify the production; for it is considered neither possible nor desirable to regulate production (by unemployment or shorter hours) so that it does no more than satisfy today's true wants. Galbraith sums the matter up as follows—

> As a society becomes increasingly affluent, wants are increasingly created by the process by which they are satisfied. This may operate passively. Increases in consumption, the counterpart of increases in production, act by suggestion or emulation to create wants. Or producers may

proceed actively to create wants through advertising and salesmanship. Wants thus come to depend on output. In technical terms it can no longer be assumed that welfare is greater at an all-round higher level of production than at a lower one. It may be the same. The higher level of production has, merely, a higher level of want creation necessitating a higher level of want satisfaction[1]

—or, still more briefly: "Production only fills a void that it has itself created." This, then, is the theoretical background to the observations in Chapter VI about the stimulation of wants by knowledge or impressions flowing in from outside. In a society dominated by the need to absorb its own production, the increase in the flow of wealth provides no more happiness or satisfaction, for the consumer must always be kept hungry for the next increase.

No doubt it will be objected that this is an extreme case. It relates, of course, to the average: that is, there must be some average level of want-creation appropriate to the growth of production (and thus of incomes), but an individual who does better than the average may still attain higher levels of satisfaction. The other side of that penny is that a person whose income increases *less* than the average will find an increasing gap opening between his stimulated wants and what he can buy; he will thus be dissatisfied, even though his income is ample to meet basic needs. The argument relates to an economy in which production is not deliberately restricted, as it has been in Britain in times of balance-of-payments trouble.

[1] *The Affluent Society*, p. 124.

Yet (as pointed out above) Britain is not free from the artificial stimulation of wants; by an infection, transmitted through the marketing professionals, she reproduces much of what goes on in the United States.

Efforts are sometimes made to turn aside the accusation of want-creation by asserting that what is being done is just to help people to discover things which they really need, so that, with the aid of informative advertising, they may live fuller and more pleasant lives. For instance, it is necessary to tell housewives how they may be freed from the drudgery of the sink by buying Fairy Liquid or Squezy: or how the children may be made happy by the use of the latest cake-mix. There is something in this argument, but it plainly does not apply over the whole field of want-stimulation. In particular, we must set on the other side the ways in which people are encouraged to feel dissatisfied (whether by advertising, or by Mrs. Jones next door) because of some trivial and perhaps wasteful change of fashion or styling.

But perhaps the process of want-creation without genuine satisfaction can be seen most clearly at work (on adults at least, and to some extent on children too) in the commercialism of the British Christmas. Every year Christmas cards multiply and become more elaborate, gift advertisements occupy more newspaper space, displays are organized early in the stores. Mrs. Jones must be given a present as good (meaning as expensive) as the one which you expect she is going to give you. Since, however, Mrs. Jones's real material needs are satiated, it is necessary to go to ever more bizarre extremes to find something original and appropriate which she has not already got. The production of unnecessary gadgets and of "gifts of character" (that is to say, gifts which no one has ever heard of, or thought of wanting, before) thrives. The period of card-posting and present-buying is extremely hard work: yet at the end of it lies a Christmas season no happier than simpler ones of past years. If this period of busy spending is a fine flower of our economic system, it is time we thought again about our purposes.

So far this chapter has been concerned with the relationship of income to happiness. It is time now to consider the effect of accumulated wealth. This, of course, is divided in a much more uneven way than income, and (if household goods, houses and capital earmarked as a provision for old age are ignored) most of the population has no significant accumulation of wealth at all. Every adult can expect to share in an income, and therefore can reasonably entertain at least a modest ambition to have a larger one; but it is not yet true that everyone can hope to be a "capitalist". We are now discussing a minority interest.

The possession of a stock of wealth in an easily realizable form can plainly yield pleasure derived from its use as income: that is to say, it can be used to supplement income, or to insure against fluctuations of income which are expected to take place. Furthermore, a stock of wealth makes it easier to show to the full that one has attained a certain status and income. Expensive cars and large houses are much more easily acquired if there is no need to borrow or to save for a long period out of income. Whereas the man with no capital behind him may find himself struggling to assert a status which his income will scarcely bear, and in consequence be discontented, the man with money in the bank or a good portfolio of securities can risk living up to the standard which he thinks appropriate to his job. The danger of discontent due to being "caught in the rat-race" is much less.

However, the status conferred by a stock of wealth is not simply derived from the use of that wealth to provide and support income. The mere fact of being known to be rich may suffice; but here we must distinguish several different examples. At one extreme is the miser, the lover of money for its own sake and not for what it can buy— except perhaps power over others. Misers are not very numerous; one supposes that they are, in a way, happy, despite the disapproval of their neighbours. At least any happiness they obtain is in their own thoughts, unconnected with questions of status in the community. At the other extreme is the spendthrift, plainly living above his income and running down his capital. He can savour the enjoyment of lavish expenditure, but not of the approval of his neighbours, who will regard his spending as denoting no permanent standing in the community. But between these two extremes the rich man can enjoy the respect due to his known riches, without the necessity of "keeping up with the Jones's". Indeed, to be counted as a man of simple life, plainly not concerned to make an outward show of wealth, is likely to enhance respect and confer a higher status. Part of the enjoyment associated with a large capital is therefore due to a status which is unassociated with income.

But much of the enjoyment is incidental. Some people just like making money. It satisfies them by showing them, to their near associates at best, to be men of ability who can wrestle with the chances and changes of the world and win. The man who has just brought off a successful deal feels like a poet who has put a good poem on paper, or a mathematician who has discovered a new theorem. It is not necessary to assume any particular enjoyment from using the money, for it is nice to be clever in the making of it. Others, again, regard their wealth as merely an incidental accompaniment to the power which they exercise over others. The ownership of a business, or better still of some great chain of businesses which dominate a market, may yield a pleasure of directing great affairs, of putting one's ideas into practice, of doing good to mankind, or of satisfying an urge to dominate others—all of which may be much more important than the cash returns. It is for a similar reason that the orthodox treatment by economists of profit is often unsatisfactory. The idea that the owners of businesses try to "maximize their profits" raises at once the question of which, of several different definitions of profit, they are attempting to maximize. If one tries to resolve this question by observation, it can quickly be seen that many business men are concerned to make such profits as will ensure the continuation, and perhaps enlargement, of their businesses. It is identification with the business which matters, an identification which matters because it enlarges the individual's power and scope: the profits are a means to this end, or perhaps just a natural accompaniment of successful activity.

Although (as pointed out in Chapter IV) provision for one's children is nowhere near as important a motive for piling up wealth as it used to be—a change which is associated with the development of economic opportunities for women, for the nineteenth-century upper-class father had to try to provide for his unmarried daughters—nevertheless there remains a limited class in which the enjoyment of a stock of wealth is strongly associated with family continuity. This is, broadly speaking, the "old aristocracy", families which have been wealthy for many generations and have acquired a sense of pride in houses, estates and other inherited possessions: but the term includes some who have no title, but come of long-settled yeoman stock or belong to one of the few substantial and long-lived family businesses. If a family has managed to maintain a certain position for centuries, through all the changes of economic and social structure that have occurred, there is an element of defiance of fate in trying to keep that position for yet another generation. Despite the effect of death duties and of high taxation of incomes, many of the families whose names are listed in *Debrett* or *Burke's Peerage* will try by sacrifice to keep the most essential of their possessions together to hand on to their children. Some fail, and some indeed are glad to retire from the struggle, because the sacrifice required is too great. Occasionally, the ranks of those who seek continuity are joined by some *nouveau riche* who sets up in a manor house or castle and entertains dreams of passing it to his eldest son.

A stock of wealth is thus enjoyable because of its implications for income and expenditure: because of the status it provides, independent of actual expenditure: because it is incidental to some other enjoyment, such as that of achievement or power: occasionally because it offers the pleasure of the prospect of family continuity. It is fair to add, however, that wealth is sometimes neutral—that is, it piles up without serving any clear purpose, simply because the interest on existing holdings exceeds the owner's desire to spend: and is occasionally a burden (just as a large income can be a burden), especially if it is associated with a form of ownership which carries onerous obligations, but cannot easily be exchanged for something simpler.

The conclusions of this chapter are not very favourable to Pigou's "unverified probability" that an increase in economic welfare, in the form of increased real income, has an effect, equivalent in direction, on the "total welfare" of an individual. There seem, on the contrary, to be many cases in which (because of the link between income and status) increases in an income which already provides for basic or absolute needs will yield no increment of happiness. In a society dominated by the desire to produce (because it is in production that men attain self-justification), and with a growing technological competence, it is necessary to ensure the creation of wants—that is, to maintain dissatisfaction despite rises in income. Our state is the unhappy one of the greyhound, chasing the electric hare which is always just beyond his reach.

For that minority which is able to accumulate or retain a significant capital, however, the picture is happier. Such people need not be troubled to the same degree in maintaining expenditure appropriate to their status: indeed, they may be able to hold their standing without need for comparable expenditure. Their ownership of wealth will often be associated with other pleasurable benefits, such as the exercise of power or the assurance of the continuity of family tradition. (I am not, of course, here suggesting that it is *desirable* that the rich man should enjoy exercising power, for the consequences may be harmful to society; I am merely making the neutral observation that such enjoyment does exist.) The instinct which leads many investors to interest themselves in capital gains rather than high income is not just a question of the relative tax treatment, or of the larger pleasure in gambling for a capital gain. There is also a reasonable belief that, if only a modest capital can be multiplied to the point at which wealth is seen to be a matter of capital rather than income, there are new advantages and pleasures to be gained. So Harrod writes of Keynes's daring speculations (he was almost bankrupt in 1920)—

... This was his fight for freedom. He had no inheritance which he could enlarge by more orthodox financial methods ... He was determined not to relapse into salaried drudgery. He must be financially independent ... These other dealers in money merely squandered their earnings on banal conventional luxuries. He must use his brains to put some of their money into his pocket, where it would fructify, not only financially, but in supporting the arts, and people who really mattered, and in giving his own powers scope.[1]

[1] *The Life of John Maynard Keynes*, p. 297.

IX

WEALTH AND CIVILIZATION

THE quotation about Keynes at the end of the last chapter is a reminder that wealth is sometimes deliberately applied to serve the higher purposes of civilization—in this case, the support of the arts: to do what Keynes himself called "encouraging, and experimenting in, the arts of life as well as the activities of purpose". We could, of course, leave the subject, as some of the older economists were satisfied to do, as an exercise in the maximization of individual happiness; but most of us would then, I think, have an ill-defined feeling that we were dodging an essential point.

It is difficult to conduct the argument in terms of a sum of individual states of happiness. Since there is no means of knowing whether assertions about states of satisfaction mean the same thing to one person as to another, it is only in exceptional and restricted circumstances that we can make meaningful assertions about an aggregate satisfaction. In particular, most conceivable economic changes make some people worse off while they make others better off, and we are therefore involved in arguments about whether the increment of satisfaction to A is more or less important than the increment of dissatisfaction to B. This problem arises even if newly discovered wealth flows to A without B, C and others being any worse off in terms of real purchasing power; for the good fortune of A may reduce the satisfaction of B, C ... by the operation of envy, that is by giving them a higher standard to live up to. Of course, a single person can make assertions about the welfare of society if he is prepared to assume that everyone else reacts in the same way as he does. This is an assumption which most of us frequently make, and it is not at all ridiculous to suppose that human beings are at least *similar* in this reaction of satisfaction and dissatisfaction. But plainly we are not identical.

Many people would wish at this point to resolve questions about the effects and importance of wealth by making a religious or quasi-religious assertion about the purpose of mankind. Thus, those who emphasize the difference between the material and spiritual worlds may see the highest purpose of men as the attainment of spiritual union with some divine and omnipresent Mind, a task which may be impeded or prevented by too much enjoyment of material things. On this view wealth, beyond the minimum necessary to keep an ascetic alive, may not only do harm to the individual but also represent a betrayal of what should be a high and common social purpose. If, on the other hand, God is seen as active in material things, as being present in the whole of creation, there is less sense of guilt associated with the use of wealth, and indeed the attainment of greater equality and the feeding of the hungry are seen as part of the task of bringing the Kingdom of Heaven to reality on earth.

In another scheme of thought, the idea of "purpose" for mankind is given no great weight: all are caught in an inevitable process, so that there is no choice of "good" or "bad" to be associated with wealth or its distribution: one just observes what is. All of these views are to be found among people who call themselves Christians, and a wider survey of other religions would disclose many variants on them.

In this book, however, I prefer to take a different line. I assume it to be a proper social aim to *advance civilization*, and this I define as making a permanent improvement to the stock of human creation, knowledge and experience. There are further explanations needed if this definition is to be meaningful. The word "permanent" carries the gloss "provided the human race has a continued existence". I assume that our present methods of preserving and multiplying the evidence of human achievement are so powerful that the likelihood of accidental loss is small, except for the danger that, as history lengthens, the sheer volume of the valuable achievement of mankind will cause some of it to be totally forgotten. Past civilizations have been largely lost from our knowledge, but this was because they left little written record or because war broke the chain of memory. But now we have films, recordings, video-tape, millions of books, great libraries, archives; it would take the destructive power of a major world war, reducing the remnants of the advanced nations to primitive subsistence, to eliminate our memory of the past.

The word "improvement" is open at once to the

criticism that there is no absolute standard by which to decide what is an improvement. Does the music of the Beatles represent an advance in civilization, or not? There is no point in pretending that an absolute definition can be given of an "advance" in the creative arts of mankind. That which is widely considered to be a valuable addition to the stock of human creations, over a period long enough to show that the judgement is more than a passing fashion, can be given probationary status as an "advance in civilization", which can be confirmed if the appreciation is repeated (though not necessarily continuous) in the future. The appreciation need not be universal—not even the Taj Mahal would be considered beautiful by everybody; and a beautiful steam engine deserves its place in the heritage of mankind, even though the love of steam engines is a minority enthusiasm. Nor need it be continuous: many great writers have suffered a period of unpopularity. The important thing is that repeated human judgement confirms the value of the advance.

Advances in knowledge are more readily identified. Every new chemical compound discovered, each new insight into the working of the human body, each exploration of a new area of Earth or the other planets, can be regarded as an "advance in civilization"; for I here assume that knowledge has a value independent of any evil use which can be made of it. (This is a value to mankind, not necessarily to particular people, who can, as suggested on page 72, have too much knowledge pressing in upon them.) As for experience, I assume again that to know what has happened in past situations is potentially valuable, though the potential is often not used.

One other gloss on the definition is needed. The creations of mankind include not only a vast range of material goods—buildings, machines, consumer goods, works of art—and a range of services, but also ways of organizing and running society. Thus the invention of parliament was an advance in civilization, and so too must be counted the great social reforms, which took a situation obviously unjust or unreasonable and altered it decisively. The attack on poverty, and moves towards greater equality, can be counted as advances. It is not necessary here to argue a theoretical case for them; it is sufficient that they are regarded, in succeeding generations, as being by common consent an improvement in civilized living. The reader must bear with a certain circularity of definition, for though civilization is recognizable (that is, we know a well-organized, educated or creative society when we see one) the word is almost incapable of being tied to a precise list of meanings.

Let me come to the doubt which has occasioned this particular way of examining the social consequences of wealth. It is the suspicion that affluence, so far from advancing civilization, may cause its decay; that in some ways greater riches produce a coarsening of appreciation, an atrophy of conscience, a tawdry glitter with no depth, a frenzied search for sensual pleasures which satisfy only for the moment. Great civilizations, it is argued, have been neither so poor that their inhabitants have been unable to raise their eyes from the struggle for existence, nor perverted by the "deceitfulness of riches". A greater flow of wealth makes a society less able to offer permanent improvements to the stock of human creation, knowledge and experience, not more. How much truth is there in this view?

Thus flatly stated, the view is plainly not tenable. The increase of factual knowledge *is* closely related to the flow of wealth. The United States, as the richest country in the world, can also support the world's largest programme of scientific research. She can and does support great numbers of scholars in the humanities and the social sciences; she builds great libraries, huge telescopes and nuclear reactors, powerful computers. While some of these actions are taken out of a desire to become still richer and of greater military power, many can be ascribed to the release of human curiosity in a situation where there is a surplus to use in trying to satisfy it. The increase of wealth is a necessary but not a sufficient condition for the existence of a great programme of discovery; it is necessary also that the habits of thinking of the community should be such as to welcome innovation rather than tradition, new thought rather than orthodoxy. It may therefore be just good fortune that the United States combines great wealth with a willingness (in matters of science and technology at least) to honour novelty.

Let us, however, consider some of the charges which

can be brought against an affluent society, and (if they seem to have validity) inquire whether any common set of causes accounts for them. I return first to the example from building on page 45. What is there said of houses applies also to many public buildings, such as our better Victorian town halls or universities. We may not like their style, nor consider them to fit modern ideas of convenience, but they are built to a standard considerably higher than that of a comparable modern building, and, though technological knowledge was less, money was well spent on solid construction, on good finishes, on appropriate embellishment, and on space ample for the original purpose of the building. Yet the country is well over twice as rich, per head, as it was in Victorian times; it might be expected to have higher standards of public building, not lower. Furthermore, although average real income per head has been rising steadily since the war, at a rate which is historically quite high (despite our economic troubles), it appears that standards for major public buildings have been further depressed, to the detriment of good architecture and with a probably harmful effect on future maintenance costs. To take another example, many of the new office blocks which disfigure our cities are not only architectural monstrosities, poorly detailed and without character, but also finished at a standard of which previous office-builders would have been ashamed. How can we account for these things?

There is, as stated on page 45, an economic explanation, namely that the cost of building has risen relatively to other goods and services. This, however, is not entirely convincing; we noted that there has been a large change in incomes as well as in relative prices, and although at present relative building prices people with Victorian incomes would no doubt economize on building standards, it does not follow that this must be so with present-day incomes. There might be a psychological explanation, namely that people now seek to demonstrate their importance and grandeur in ways other than building; but this is really a rephrasing of the problem rather than an answer to it. The discussion in previous chapters, however, has suggested other explanations. One is that the stimulation of new desires has gone on faster than the growth of wealth, so that, instead of feeling that we have a greater margin to spend on doing the job really well, we are under stronger pressure to secure economies. Another aspect of the matter is that we have become more sophisticated in quantifying the benefits of our actions. Space in a building which is there purely to provide architectural style, that is, which "does not earn its keep", therefore tends to be eliminated. But we are not yet sophisticated enough to get a right balance of present and future costs; because the future is uncertain, and we are tempted to let our successors take care of themselves, we sacrifice solid, lasting construction and "easy-care" finishes to present cheapness. This is one aspect of the tendency, mentioned on page 49, to take short views.

It is, indeed, sometimes argued that we should make a virtue of shortsightedness, because we ought not to inflict on our grandchildren (whose ideas of good building will be different) the creations which happen to satisfy us. Therefore built-in obsolescence can be represented as an advantage. The ideal building would maintain perfect finish for sixty years, and then fall down instantaneously, breaking into fragments of a convenient size to take away. The fact that, by building for a sixty-year life, we probably ensure that evidence of decay will show much earlier is inconvenient and regrettable, but nothing should be done about it.

This attitude to building, particularly in the public sector, is a symptom of a disease of affluence with wider consequences. Since, above all, production must be maintained and increased, there is no longer a stigma attached to early obsolescence and decay. It is not yet quite respectable to admit that it is an aim of business to make things which will not last, but we have become accustomed to lower standards of construction in many of our goods. This is not necessarily always a bad thing—one could claim that civilization is advanced by introducing more frequent changes—but the general effect, in driving down standards of craftsmanship and in causing attention to superficial attractiveness rather than lasting fitness for use, can only be regarded as lost ground.

To see how much ground has been lost, consider some of the examples given by Vance Packard in *The Waste Makers*, a book written in 1960 about the wastefulness of the American economy. Much of what he describes has within a few years become familiar in Britain also. For instance, he quotes from *Design News* that a "highly placed engineer" in a portable-radio company had stated that his product was designed to last not more than three years: on which the editor of that paper commented—

> Is purposeful design for product failure unethical? The particular engineer in question stoutly defends his company's design philosophy in two ways: first, if portable radios characteristically lasted ten years, the market might be saturated long before repeat sales could support continued volume manufacturing . . . ; second, the user would be denied benefits of accelerated progress if long life is a product characteristic.

He reports a large maker of men's clothing happily reporting "that men had been given an entirely different look in a mere five years . . . With the rapid acceleration of new models the industry was finally achieving the style obsolescence it had so long sought". He discusses the deliberate styling obsolescence of cars, but also various examples of low quality: for instance, he quotes from a survey by Consumers' Research—

> There seems to be no doubt that bodies of present-day cars could be made to last much longer than they now do, but manufacturers are fully aware that if they make their cars too durable, future sales will suffer . . .

Cars were still being built with mufflers (that is, silencers) which required replacement on an average every two years at a cost to the consumer of $18 to $27: but the cost of using materials which would last the life of the car was estimated to be an additional 8 cents. But these, and the many other examples given, can all be blamed on the consumer: Mr. Louis Cheskin is quoted as saying—

> Why make the handles on cups so that they won't break off? Who wants to pay 10 per cent more for dishes so that the dishes will last a lifetime? Most housewives want or welcome an excuse to buy a new set of dishes every year or so. Who wants furniture to last for ever? ... Furniture, clothes, dishes can all be made to last longer at very little additional cost. But neither the maker nor the consumer is interested in this.

With the tendency to take the benefits of greater wealth in the form of variety, even if this implies a loss of quality, goes a vast wastefulness. This is seen, for instance, in unnecessary packaging; in making things so that they cannot be used to the full (for example, the contents of some aerosol cans) and putting them in containers which cannot be re-used; and in persuading the consumer to engage in unnecessary duplication—like having sets of colour-matched underwear to suit the female's various moods. It is nice to know that as far back as 1960 the Plumbing Fixture Manufacturers Association in the United States was promoting the "privazone home". This is one in which each member of the family has a private water closet.

It is no use dismissing this kind of thing with a smile as mere United States ebullience, for Britain and other advanced countries are far along the same path. Those who make things are not often to be found consciously injuring their interests by making them too well—though perhaps a word of congratulation should go to the makers of men's socks, who both in Britain and the United States appear to have done severe damage to their prospects by lengthening the life of their product! Our great-grandmothers bought toys for the children which withstood the use of several generations; now it is common for toys to be thrown aside, broken, after a few days. But is our feeling, that in this change something good has been lost, any more than a nostalgia for a now unnecessary craftsmanship?

The reason for thinking that a more serious decline in the quality of civilization is involved is that the waste, planned obsolescence and excessive variety exist in a world most of whose inhabitants are still poor, and whose resources are limited. "The very trimming of the vain world would clothe all the naked one" wrote William Penn: and again, "Were frugality universal we should be cured of two extremes, want and excess. And the one would supply the other and so bring both nearer to a mean, the just degree of earthly happiness. It is a reproach to religion and government to suffer so much poverty and excess." These phrases come from his work, *Some Fruits of Solitude*, published in 1693; but the problem of the coexistence of waste and poverty was of great concern to him earlier, as he lay imprisoned in the Tower of London in 1668. "Truly it is a reproach to a man" he wrote (in *No Cross, No Crown*) "that he knows not when he hath enough; when to leave off; when to be satisfied." He saw little true satisfaction in affluence, and speaks eloquently of the hardships of those who seek money (see page 92)—

Is this to live comfortably, or to be rich? Do we not see how early they rise; how late they go to bed? how full of the Change, the Shop, the Warehouse, the Custom-house; of bills, bonds, charter-parties, etc. they are?—running up and down, as if it were to save the life of a condemned innocent.

But his main practical conclusion was as follows—

That if the money which is expended in every parish in such vain fashions, as wearing of laces, jewels, embroideries, unnecessary ribbons, trimming, costly furniture and attendance, together with what is commonly consumed in taverns, feasts, gaming, etc. could be collected into a Public Stock, or something in lieu of this extravagant and fruitless expense, there might be reparation to the broken tenants, work-houses for the able, and almshouses for the aged and impotent. Then should we have no beggars in the land, the cry of the widow and the orphan would cease . . .

The reader may perhaps judge this quaint passage to be mere kill-joy Puritanism, and doubt whether in the seventeenth century the "vain world" was in fact large enough to yield from its trimming the clothing of the naked one. The general relief of poverty may have been then, as it remains now, an unattainable ideal in most of the countries of the world. But Penn's words relate more directly to our present condition. To have achieved the disposable paper dress, the electric toothbrush, the throw-away container in a world still largely poor, and to expect the extension of affluence to mean a constant struggle to create new desires in those already well above subsistence level, is surely a symptom of decline in the quality of civilization. Penn condemned a small rich minority of his time: but what shall we say when a whole nation is rich enough to give each of its members far more than they need for subsistence?

In other words, concern about social justice and the distribution of wealth is an essential part of the quality of a civilization, and should be the more expected of a nation as its wealth increases and the possibility of doing something effective to relieve poverty becomes greater. It is usual for advanced nations nowadays to congratulate themselves, both on the comprehensiveness of the welfare benefits provided within their boundaries, and on the generosity of their overseas aid. Yet have we so much to be proud about? Detailed studies of welfare services in Britain, for instance, still reveal considerable areas of genuine hardship, and instances of official inflexibility which would have been considered disgraceful by a Relieving Officer of the old-style Poor Law Guardians. The distribution of available income has of course been forcibly made more equal by taxation, but this does not necessarily justify the range which remains, nor must we forget that a large share of indirect taxation is carried by the poor. As for foreign aid, it has to be seen against the background of the great benefits which the advanced industrial nations have obtained over recent periods, at the expense of the poor producers of raw materials and food, because of the depression of the prices of these primary products relative to manufactured goods.

There is not, in fact, much evidence that the spirit of

Good King Wenceslas or Mr. Cheeryble is increasingly active among wealthy men and nations. Within those nations, the danger may rather be an increasing indifference to social problems because we believe that they have already been solved. "No one is poor nowadays" we say "or if they are, it is their own fault." Yet the existence of a satisfactory average standard of living (allowing the various forms of waste mentioned above) does not excuse us from looking at the extreme cases. Poor Sissy, in Dickens's *Hard Times*, found it impossible to persuade Mr. M'Choakumchild of this elementary point—

"And he said, Now, this schoolroom is a Nation. And in this nation, there are fifty millions of money. Isn't this a prosperous nation? Girl number twenty, isn't this a prosperous nation, and arn't you in a thriving state?"

"What did you say?" asked Louisa.

"Miss Louisa, I said I didn't know. I thought I couldn't know whether it was a prosperous nation or not, and whether I was in a thriving state or not, unless I knew who had got the money, and whether any of it was mine. But that had nothing to do with it. It was not in the figures at all", said Sissy, wiping her eyes.

"That was a great mistake of yours", observed Louisa.

"Yes, Miss Louisa, I know it was, now. Then Mr. M'Choakumchild said he would try me again. And he said, This schoolroom is an immense town, and in it there are a million of inhabitants, and only five-and-twenty are starved to death in the streets, in the course of a year. What is your remark on that proportion? And my remark was—for I couldn't think of a better one—that I thought it must be just as hard upon those who starved, whether the others were a million, or a million million. And that was wrong, too."

The other aspect of the wasteful habits of affluence which should cause us concern, but seldom does so, is our prodigal use of the world's resources of (for instance) fuels, metals and timber. It is said that the United States alone has used more raw materials in forty years than the whole of humanity in all preceding generations up to 1914. We protect ourselves from the uncomfortable implications of such a fact by supposing that science will somehow get us out of any future difficulties. Yet it cannot be assumed as self-evident that substitute raw materials will be *both* as good *and* as cheap. And even they have to be made from something, and the "something" is not always a neglected raw material in ample supply—the substitute may merely increase pressure in an area where the use of resources is already excessive. It can, I suppose, be offered as an excuse that earlier generations were equally ready to let posterity take care of itself. But it was one thing to take no thought for the future when the world's population was small, and the rate of exploitation of resources small also; it is another thing to continue with the same attitude as both population and the rate of exploitation rise steeply, and a significant part of the extra demand is for purposes which can claim no urgency or necessity. The quality of the civilization of affluence is again too well described by the slogan "I'm all right, Jack."

Among the assets which society lays waste in the search for wealth is natural beauty. I use this term in a loose sense, because much of what we call "natural beauty" is, in fact, man-made. The rural landscape of Britain is not primeval forest, but the green pastures, fertile fields, hedgerows and walls created by many generations of farming. The sense of harmony which it conveys is the consequence, partly of the beauty of its separate elements, partly of the softening influence of time on any incongruities which man introduces, and partly of the good taste of past generations in keeping those incongruities to a minimum. Into the harmony of the landscape, the Industrial Revolution introduced the major incongruity of industrial waste and dereliction. We are gradually learning how to deal with these, though both are still spreading in many areas. The rise of population, the greater amount of space which a more wealthy population demands, and the needs of transport have made large further inroads into unspoilt areas. There is little point in complaining of losses which are inevitable. What is a matter for concern is that, notwithstanding planning controls, the visual quality of so many of the changes is low. Despite great improvements in education, it is not possible to rely on the good taste and common sense of the population to prevent atrocious interference with the beauty of our surroundings. Why is this?

One reason, no doubt, is that a wealthy society is obsessed with wealth and its creation, and tends to underrate the importance of things to which no money value can readily be given. Present-day industrialists, just like their predecessors, sometimes explain that the ugliness they create is the inevitable accompaniment of their processes—by which they mean that, since beauty has no clear value to them, it is not worth while spending a small part of their profits on the prevention of ugliness. Furthermore, rich societies are commonly mobile, which means that men are less afraid of the judgement of their fellows and less conscious of a continuing obligation to a local community. But the destruction of beauty may be associated also with the general tendency to short views (page 49), the toleration of waste, and the familiarity with the crude assertive practices of advertising. The need of the individual business man to shriek out his assertions of importance, so as to drown his rivals, is often a cause of ugliness.

It is convenient at this point to pick up the observation on page 114 about the paradox that we try to obtain more economies as we grow richer, because the stimulation of new desires runs ahead of our ability to satisfy them. This, too, is relevant to our attitude to natural beauty. The adjustment of our new creations to their surroundings costs money. Occasionally we spend it, as in the landscaping of the motorways, but more often the finer adjustments are eliminated in favour of what is more directly functional. It would not be regarded as at all natural to suggest that, since this year we are two or three per cent more wealthy than last, we can afford to spend more on the prevention of ugliness or on removing the evidence of past misdeeds. Progress is slowly made, by defining and imposing standards (for example, of smoke control, for smoke is a major cause of ugliness); but the slowness is always a matter of "not enough money", by which we mean "too many other things to do".

The matter of water supply from the Lake District provides an excellent test problem on the quality of our civilization. Manchester Corporation, supplying large areas of the North-west, needs further supplies of water. These could come from many different sources—or the need could be reduced (at a cost) by greater attention to the recirculation of existing water. Of the sources of new supplies, the Lake District, with heavy and consistent rainfall and reservoirs almost ready made in the lakes or dry valleys, is the most convenient and probably the cheapest. It can also be exploited more quickly than some other sources, which means that, if decisions are deferred long enough, the use of further Lake District sources may become almost inevitable because all the alternatives will be too slow. It can reasonably be argued that the interference with natural beauty will be fairly small, that some of it will be only a temporary scarring, and that even a regulated man-made lake can be a thing of beauty. The difficulties about freedom of access to reservoirs and their gathering grounds seem to be much less than they used to be. The economic arguments in favour of allowing further exploitation of Lake District sources thus seem very strong: the counter-arguments lack the convincing support of estimates in hard cash. With growing wealth, we need more water; here is an economical source; the effect on beauty is no worse than with other man-made changes which we tolerate—for example the widening of roads.

Against this one can only argue that two blacks do not make a white: that an area like the Lake District is held in trust for mankind and for future generations; that, with all its associations, it is unique, and we should no more interfere with it, without need, than we would splash fresh paint on the *Mona Lisa*. Such an assertion of absolute priority needs to be made with care. Some may prefer to say that "nothing is sacred", but nevertheless give to this particular natural asset a strong presumption of priority because of its high importance. A more wealthy society should be better able to concede this priority, but in fact (if the preceding analysis is right) is likely to develop habits of mind which resist this concession. If Manchester water goes up in cost, because another source has to be developed, this is a clearly seen and quantifiable disadvantage, occurring here and now. A loss of unique natural beauty is a disadvantage which might not be greatly noticed, and (though nominally it would fall on future generations) how can people regret what they have never known? Yet the loss would be a permanent lowering of the quality of human experience. A civilized society would prevent it, and bear the consequent cost. I believe that an affluent society is unlikely to agree to do so.

This chapter has so far argued that, though wealth contributes to the quality of civilization by making possible more research and better education (possibilities which can be realized if other favourable factors are present), it also tends to subtract from it for several reasons. These include the accompanying excessive stimulation of new desires: the tendency to short views: the acceptance of planned obsolescence and waste: and the respect given to financial benefits, as against those which cannot readily be counted in money terms. I do not, however, simply because the advanced nations are becoming richer, wish to attribute to their riches all the troubles of the day. For instance, the time is one of great confusion in the creative arts, and many find it hard to establish a clear standard of what is good and what is bad, so that they give as their judgements what they think will be popular with their listeners, without any depth of conviction. There are aspects of contemporary art and music to which it would be reasonable to attach the adjective "decadent", or even "fraudulent": some represent a throw-back to crude experience in a primitive society, and thus a decline in civilization, while some developments seem little more than an exploitation of a credulous public which has no clear standards of its own. But these features may be the consequence of war and international insecurity, of the rapidity of technological change, of some law of the ageing of civilizations, of the decline of religion, or any of a dozen possible "causes" which, while interrelated with growing wealth, are not solely a consequence of it.

There is, however, one consequence for our culture of increasing wealth which is immediate and deserves notice.

This is the growth of a mass market for popular music, popular art-forms, and popular literature, in which considerable sums of money can be made and in which, as a consequence, the techniques of demand-creation are employed in a sophisticated way. There is plainly a relevant cultural change in the mere fact that what was formerly a matter for a small group of educated patrons has now become the subject of mass patronage. For instance, those who through the last three hundred years have acted as patrons of classical European music have had a broad historical knowledge of their subject, which has tended to preserve the continuity of tradition. Modern "pop" music has no such links with past forms; it can experiment, using sounds which are technologically new, in the creation of new sensations and experiences. It would be snobbish to suppose that this must automatically be deplored. But behind the music which can be sold on millions of discs throughout the world stand shrewd business men, who are not interested to produce better music so much as music which will sell, by catching the latest movement of fashion or creating a new fashion by careful propaganda. Material of very variable quality— one is tempted to say, of almost any quality—can successfully be promoted into the Top Twenty; and there is enough money in popular success to justify heavy promotion expenses. The same factors can be seen at work in the promotion of certain bookstall paperbacks, which (despite an absence of any great literary merit) sell in millions all over the world. Allied to this, again, is the debasement of culture by the commercial exploitation of interest in sex, whether in its ordinary or its perverse forms. It sometimes seems, as a consequence, that even good literature has become difficult to sell unless it can be decorated with a nude torso, or in some other way made to suggest a sexual or sadistic interest.

So likewise the contents of our television programmes, particularly in those countries where they are open to commercial sponsorship, are heavily influenced by the fact that there is money in sex and violence. This may not do us as much harm as is sometimes feared, for stylized violence on television does not engage the emotions, any more than a murder in a detective story. But it certainly does not represent an advance in civilization—a permanent improvement in the stock of human creation. The discovery that there is money in music, art, writing, broadcasting of a certain kind is likely to be harmful to culture and to civilization, because it causes a preoccupation with the types of art in which money can most readily be made, and a use of propaganda to manipulate and change people's judgements.

A quite different possible effect of increasing wealth on the quality of civilization must now be considered, namely its effect on the quality of the human race. The argument runs as follows. Men develop their faculties and talents, and broaden their understanding and appreciation, in part by the process of meeting and overcoming difficulties: provided that the difficulties are not so overwhelmingly great that vision is narrowed by fatigue and

unremitting toil. If, by becoming richer, we arrive
eventually at the Garden of Eden, we shall find it a poor
place to build character or culture. Without exercise in
a struggle for existence, man will fail to come to his full
potential: without knowledge of great tragedy and great
achievement, he will be unable to create great art: without need of sympathy in adversity, he will be less sensitive
of spirit and will become incapable of deep appreciation.
Putting the matter crudely, the highest human achievements come neither when a man is starving and desperate,
nor when he is well-fed and indolent. Beyond a certain
point, therefore, increasing wealth is likely to mean the
decline and decadence of civilization—decadence because,
lacking a natural stimulation of his higher qualities, man
will resort to an artificial stimulation of animal enjoyment.

Though it is natural to distrust broad generalizations,
this one has a certain ring of truth. We have to be careful
not to be led astray by sentimentality about the past; our
forefathers were not all honest, hard-working yeomen of
sterling quality. We need care, too, in generalizing about
the present; after all, a large section of the present
generation was exposed to the special difficulties of war.
This is perhaps one special reason for lack of sympathy
between the old and the young: those who experienced
the Great Depression and the Second World War cannot
imagine that those who never had this experience can be
of the same quality, and this may be a form of envy.
However, there is enough evidence in general human
experience to suggest that some, at least, of the qualities

which we recognize as making a civilization fine have their origin in adversity. It is difficult to imagine great literature without tragedy: great music written by a composer who has never been stretched in spirit by exposure to varied difficulties in his own or his neighbour's experience: a full intellectual achievement, in a world which no longer has an urgent practical need for achievement and is motivated only by curiosity. It is not unreasonable, too, to relate the craving for new sensations of body and mind, which in the advanced countries leads to experimentation with drugs, to a lack of satisfaction in the stimulation provided by the environment.

All this (you will say) is old hat. Notice, however, that I am not entering into the age-old argument about the value and effects of suffering. Adversity and difficulty may or may not be related to suffering. My discussion relates to the effect on human beings of working against adverse circumstances—that is, circumstances which are moderately but not overwhelmingly adverse. A hopeless struggle is certainly productive of suffering, but one which is merely difficult may yield the pleasures of achievement. I am not therefore saying that civilization is improved by making people unhappy: only that it is improved by not making things too easy.

This argument will remind some readers of Samuel Smiles' *Self-Help*; and this is no bad thing, for, despite the tendency to regard Smiles as a quaint Victorian figure, much of his work speaks very directly to our present condition. He was in no doubt about the effect of wealth on character—

An easy and luxurious existence does not train men to effort or encounter with difficulty; nor does it awaken that consciousness of power which is so necessary for energetic and effective action in life. Indeed, so far from poverty being a misfortune, it may, by vigorous self-help, be converted even into a blessing; rousing a man to that struggle with the world in which, though some may purchase ease by degradation, the right-minded and true-hearted find strength, confidence and triumph.[1]

The youth who inherits wealth is apt to have life made too easy for him, and he soon grows sated with it, because he has nothing left to desire. Having no special object to struggle for, he finds time hang heavy on his hands; he remains morally and spiritually asleep; and his position in society is often no higher than that of a polypus over which the tide floats.

> His only labour is to kill the time,
> And labour dire it is, and weary woe.[2]

"Man owes his growth" he wrote "chiefly to that active striving of the will, that encounter with difficulty, which we call effort." His book is a long series of examples to illustrate this theme. He was a good Victorian in thinking in terms of individuals, and not of societies or civilizations, but his view was not limited to examples of worldly success. His examples of energy in overcoming difficulty include Napoleon and Wellington, Warren Hastings and Charles Napier, but also St. Francis Xavier, Dr. Livingstone, Granville Sharp the pioneer of the abolition of

---

[1] *Self-Help*, centenary edition, 1958, pp. 50-1.   [2] ibid., p. 299.

slavery, Thomas Clarkson and Fowell Buxton, Michel-
angelo, John Dalton—in fact, a great company from
every area of human culture and intellectual achievement. He quotes a judge who, when asked what contri-
buted most to success at the bar, replied "some succeed
by great talent, some by high connexions, some by
miracle, but the majority by commencing without a
shilling!" Difficulty stimulates quality: "it is not good
that human nature should have the road of life made too
easy."

If this view is accepted, it has the unwelcome, perhaps
even paradoxical, implication that the hope of creating
a Utopia or Heaven on earth, by the multiplication of
material goods until all material needs are satisfied and
time is set free for higher achievement, is automatically
self-frustrating. It is of no use to sing Addington Sy-
monds' hymn—

> These things shall be! A loftier race
> Than e'er the world hath known, shall rise
> With flame of freedom in their souls
> And light of science in their eyes . . .
>
> New arts shall bloom of loftier mould,
> And mightier music thrill the skies,
> And every life shall be a song,
> When all the earth is paradise.

The most we must hope for, if the quality of civilization
is to be maintained, is a continued struggle against perpetual difficulty. Fortunately, so far as our economic
circumstances are concerned, the growth in the number

of the human race seems likely in due course to provide that difficulty.

I have heard it argued that a sufficient degree of adversity is assured by our inability to prevent death: so that even the wealthiest society never has the ultimate ease of immortality for its members. But, since death is inevitable, there is no point in struggling against its ultimate occurrence. If it is the struggle, rather than the difficulty, which matters, the continued existence of death is irrelevant. It is possible that the *postponement* of death (see page 50), so that those in the middle years of life in the advanced countries regard it as a very unlikely occurrence (whereas a few centuries ago the thought of death was near to men throughout their life), has had an effect on human sensibility, and perhaps particularly on attitudes to religion. But we neither can turn this clock back, nor would wish to.

It can be claimed that in recent times war has provided the adverse circumstances needed to stimulate the human race. The ingenious satire of *Report from Iron Mountain* makes the point in various forms—

> [Until new political machinery is developed] the continuance of the war system must be assured, if for no other reason . . . than to preserve whatever quality and degree of poverty a society requires as an incentive . . .
>
> The most obvious of these [sociological] functions is the time-honoured use of military institutions to provide anti-social elements with an acceptable role in the social structure . . .
>
> War provides . . . for the dissipation of general boredom,

one of the most consistently undervalued and unrecognized of social phenomena . . .

But modern war is so large and unpredictable an event that its ill effects cannot be controlled and brought into relation to any good it may do. War is liable to produce overwhelmingly adverse circumstances, depressing or destroying the quality of civilization. Apologists sometimes point to the valuable results of *playing* at war—that is, of general peace-time conscription. There is, however, no way of ensuring that the operation remains a matter of play or social ritual.

Another hope of establishing Utopia is offered by those who believe, first that increasing wealth offers new opportunities of civilization (for instance, resources sufficient to build opera houses, rescue creative artists from unsuitable toil, and establish new and higher standards of social justice): and, second, that the human need to overcome difficulty can be met because human desires are indefinitely extensible. The first of these points is valid. Rich countries can certainly build opera houses: the doubts here explored are concerned with whether they will also have great composers of opera. The second point is more doubtful. Making people desire things (because there is wealth available to get them) is not the same as convincing people that the things they desire are really important. I take liberty to doubt whether the quality of experience in overcoming the difficulties of producing a mink-lined lavatory seat is equivalent to that enjoyed in producing food. What the extensibility of human desire can ensure is that (as we have seen on pages 62 and 87) people will always be dissatisfied, and therefore anxious to go on working to earn more money. But I do not find it very plausible to suppose that the quality of civilization can be supported indefinitely by the forced stimulation of a needless dissatisfaction.

This chapter therefore seems to come to a conclusion as discouraging as the last. There is a presumption that, while increasing wealth improves certain opportunities for civilized activity, it also damages the prospects of civilization in a number of ways, possibly including an impairment of certain qualities in the human beings who form the civilization. But nothing which has been said, in this chapter or the last, implies exact mechanistic connexions. The production of more wealth, in a world which still contains much real poverty, cannot be of itself evil. What we have to do is to find ways of overcoming or minimizing the harmful effects, whether on the satisfaction of individuals or on the quality of the civilization in which they live. These practical implications for policy are the subject of my final chapter.

X

IMPLICATIONS FOR POLICY

IF you look back to Chapter I, you will see that I was there arguing that comparisons of measures of wealth need to be interpreted with great care if they are not to overstate the true differences in welfare. The argument of the later chapters suggests that the difficulty is more serious than the statisticians have realized, for it is conceivable that, beyond subsistence level, quite large differences in wealth can occur with little or no improvement in individual welfare or in the quality of a civilization. The first implication for policy, therefore, is that in the advanced countries we should cease to regard the increase in the national product as being a self-evident first priority, or a principal test of economic effectiveness. This might produce considerable technological unemployment among growth-theory economists, who can perhaps be persuaded to turn their minds to the consideration of what economics really ought to be about.

However, the abandonment of economic growth as a prime object would not be at all easy. A country as rich as the United States ought to be able to give its attention to the distribution of the wealth which it already possesses, and to its aid to the rest of the world. But there are poor people in the United States, and much the easiest way of helping them is to have an all-round increase in wealth. The alternative, of making rich people poorer in order to level up those who are poor, is regarded as unattractive by the rich, who are in most countries not without influence. However, an all-round increase in wealth is liable to be achieved by the agency of a general stimulation of dissatisfaction, so that at the end of the process no one is any happier, and the gap between rich and poor yawns as widely as ever.

It will always seem that one more increase in national wealth is worth while, not only for the sake of the poor, but because of the indefinite extensibility of public services. *Ex ante*, it will always appear desirable to have wider roads, more elaborate medical services, more spacious schools. Furthermore, the whole economic system is designed for growth, and it will be difficult to maintain its efficiency if it is not subject to the constant stimulation of increases in demand. However, this difficulty is one which will have to be faced, at least in countries with a slowly changing population. Geometric progressions cannot go on for ever in a finite world. It may be sensible to try to double the British standard of living in twenty-five years, but it is not sensible to multiply it by sixteen in a century—or even to multiply it by five, by additions each quarter-century equal to our present income. Some time, the growth of income per head must flatten out.

By suggesting the possible abandonment of *general* growth as an object of policy, I am not of course arguing that there should be *no* growth or change. There are plenty of things to put right, even in the most advanced countries; in particular, there are public services which genuinely need development. I am, however, suggesting a conclusion which is only conditionally favourable to the sacred doctrine of Consumer Sovereignty. At present, an improvement in public services is extracted, with much difficulty and grumbling, from a public which is readily persuaded to engage in all sorts of quite unnecessary expenditure. The freedom of the public to spend an increase of income on bingo, beer, or plastic gnomes for the garden is regarded as absolute, and nothing is more offensive to true lovers of freedom than a suggestion that someone (presumably a faceless civil servant) is deciding on behalf of the community that some kinds of expenditure are more important than others.

There is an element of humbug about this. Centrally determined priorities of expenditure have long existed—some things being heavily taxed while some are subsidized, and some bought by the public purse from money forcibly raised by taxation. The sovereignty of the consumer is not the sovereignty of independent judgement exercised on good and complete information, but rather the response to pressures of propaganda in a situation of partial ignorance. The freedom to spend our money as we wish is worth preserving, *provided* two conditions are met: first, that we allocate enough to essential public purposes not purchasable in the market: and, second, that care is taken to make our choices as factual and sensible as possible. The freedom to be influenced to buy a branded drug, instead of an equivalent in the British Pharmacopoea at a quarter of the price, is not worth fighting for.

In order to make progress in deciding what the aims of policy should be, it will be necessary to have some sort of definition of what is "essential". No such definition can be precise, for we cannot abstract altogether from what is tolerable and technically possible *in a given society*. For instance, it is not sensible to assume that all the houses in the country can suddenly shrink to a minimum size. We must accept what exists. Even from a physiological point of view, the definition of a basic minimum diet is now seen to be much more complicated than a crude count of calories and protein content; and we have to consider also the fact that "variety is the spice of life"— a serious loss of satisfaction is involved in a diet which is too monotonous, a fact of which many would-be slimmers can speak with feeling. The austere standard of poverty which Seebohm Rowntree used in his first study of York (*Poverty: a Study of Town Life*, 1901) provided nothing at all for amusements, nor even for newspapers or trade union subscriptions.[1] Even on this standard,

[1] "A family living upon the scale allowed for in this estimate must never spend a penny on railway fare or omnibus. They must never go into the country unless they walk. They must never purchase a halfpenny newspaper or spend a penny to buy a ticket for a popular concert. They must write no letters to absent children, for they cannot afford to pay the postage. They must never contribute anything to

nearly ten per cent of the whole population of York were living in poverty. It is the almost complete disappearance of such absolute poverty which creates the new situation which gives rise to this book. Yet (as pointed out on page 62), once we get away from standards of absolute physiological necessity, we slide into a world of pure relativity, in which things are "essential" simply because most other people have got them.

Difficult as it is, the attempt must be made. It is perhaps easier in an advanced country to begin from the examination of the standard of living of a family which plainly has enough to eat, adequate clothing and satisfactory house-room, and consider what items in the family's expenditure could be eliminated or reduced without loss of physical efficiency or opportunity of cultural or intellectual development. (This is not the same as "without loss of enjoyment"; the depression of a family below the standard of its neighbours would lead to loss of enjoyment even if the things lost were quite inessential.) The "subsistence level" thus derived would be a zone of uncertainty, not a precise point, and it will be necessary to widen the zone to allow for inefficiency in the spending of income; for none of us, whatever our education or

---

their Church or Chapel, or give any help to a neighbour which costs them money. They cannot save, nor can they join sick club or Trade Union, because they cannot pay the necessary subscriptions. The children must have no pocket money for dolls, marbles or sweets. The father must smoke no tobacco, and must drink no beer . . . Should a child fall ill, it must be attended by the parish doctor; should it die, it must be buried by the parish." (*Poverty*, pp. 133–4.)

experience, can be sure always to pick up good bargains or to make purchasing decisions wisely.

Let it be assumed, then, that (for a particular country and period) we have defined a subsistence level; for Britain it might turn out to be at or somewhat above the level of social security benefits. It then becomes possible to calculate what excess exists, beyond providing for the subsistence of the population, and to direct attention to the ways in which this excess is used and ought to be used. More precisely, the gross national product can be seen as providing for—

Investment at home and overseas
Government expenditure which yields direct benefit
Government expenditure on "regrettable necessities" or on overcoming difficulties and complications in the country concerned
The subsistence of consumers
The excess expenditure of consumers

and we can direct attention to the way in which the excess is in fact distributed. Does everyone get as much as the subsistence level? Is the remainder evenly or unevenly distributed?

The first virtue of this approach is that it would enable us to begin to think straight about differences between nations. Consider, for instance, a statement such as the following—

In 1950 and 1959 the real product per head of Britain was exceeded only by that of the United States, Canada and Sweden: but by 1967 we had also been passed by Norway, France, West Germany and the Netherlands.

This is the sort of statement which is designed to make us feel miserable and ashamed. But what does it mean, if our interest is in the satisfaction of individuals or the quality of civilization? Do we suffer from a greater incidence of absolute poverty? Is the satisfaction received from the excess over the subsistence level greater or less? (About sixty-five per cent of the domestic product of the U.K. goes to private consumption, but only fifty-seven per cent in Germany.)[1] What part of Government expenditure is yielding direct benefit or enjoyments and what part is due to military commitments or adventures, or merely offsets adverse circumstances? (Public consumption takes twenty-one per cent of the domestic product of the U.S.A., seventeen per cent for the U.K., but only thirteen per cent for France.)[2] We must get ourselves into the habit of considering this kind of detail— and also of remembering that the statistics themselves are not precise, and are open to the variations of definition outlined in Chapter I: so that what we are offered is not a single and unequivocal comparison, but a whole selection of different ones, with various errors attached to them.

The second advantage would be to force us to think about the distribution of resources not required for subsistence, and to consider whether there are ways of

[1] OECD *Economic Outlook*, December 1967, quoted in *National Institute Economic Review*, February 1968: percentages relate to 1966.
[2] ibid.

influencing this distribution which will increase individual satisfaction or maintain the values of civilization.
There are some who, perceiving the problem of getting
a right balance of expenditure, once the point of minimum subsistence is passed, see the answer in the return
of more public services to the private sector, so that
rational choices can be made by individual consumers.
If we then get the answer wrong, it will be our own
fault. The disadvantage of this approach is its limited
applicability. Education could just conceivably be re-
turned wholly to the private sector, but not the drains,
nor the parks, nor (I suspect) the public libraries. As long
as a substantial public sector of spending exists, there is
really no alternative to engaging in rational thought
about the pattern of the total use of resources. Otherwise,
we are in danger of the imbalance, somewhat exagger-
atedly described by Galbraith—

The family which takes its mauve and cerise, air-con-
ditioned, power-steered, and power-braked car out for a
tour passes through cities that are badly paved, made
hideous by litter, blighted buildings, bill-boards, and posts
for wires that should long since have been put under-
ground. They pass on into a countryside that has been
rendered largely invisible by commercial art. (The goods
which the latter advertises have an absolute priority in our
value system. Such aesthetic considerations as a view of
the countryside accordingly come second. On such matters
we are consistent.) They picnic on exquisitely packaged
food from a portable icebox by a polluted stream and go
on to spend the night at a park which is a menace to

public health and morals. Just before dozing off on an air-mattress, beneath a nylon tent, amid the stench of decaying refuse, they may reflect vaguely on the curious unevenness of their blessings. Is this, indeed, the American genius?[1]

There are other ways in which the statisticians can help us to get a wiser understanding of our true condition, apart from directing attention to the surplus over subsistence level. In Chapter VII I have suggested that there may be disadvantages in having too many published statistical indicators, and that improvements of quality and presentation are more important than an increase in the number of available figures. I may perhaps be permitted to underline the point by quotation from a book which I wrote, jointly with Mr. A. D. Roy, in 1953; though at that time I would have been counted among those who think that you cannot have too many statistics—

There is clearly a need for presenting certain important statistics in a form that enables their import to be easily digested by the intelligent non-technician.

Important statistics should have attached to them some discussion of the errors to which, *a priori*, they would seem likely to be subject. Often these errors are only known by the statistician who prepares the figures, and later users may be misled by a spurious appearance of accuracy . . . Subjective estimates of error (for example, grouping of estimates into classes according to their quality) should be made whenever quantitative investigations are

[1] *The Affluent Society*, pp. 196–7.

impossible, and these subjective estimates should be published.

Where a suspected bias is corrected, the correction should be explicitly stated, so that it will be open to further investigation and criticism.

We cannot help feeling that a more imaginative approach to statistics would result in more use of techniques designed to give *relevant* answers *quickly*—as, for instance, by specially designed sample inquiries.[1]

In the past fifteen years (since this book was published) some improvements in the presentation of statistics have been achieved; but I suspect that the net movement has been backwards rather than forwards. There has been an increase in quantity: no doubt an improvement in the quality of many figures, with improving expertise, though there are areas in which quality has declined because the administrative controls which originally yielded the figures are no longer operative; but explanation has not increased in proportion to the increase of the quantity of information released. The recommendation quoted above, about the attachment of a discussion of errors, remains almost wholly ignored. Furthermore, statisticians tend to regard "presentation" as a tidying-up of tables, and "explanation" as a set of footnotes explaining definitions. What is badly needed is more *interpretation*, by people who handle the figures from day to day and know what weight they can bear and what hidden snares lie in wait for the user. The quantity of such

[1] *British Economic Statistics*, C. F. CARTER and A. D. ROY, pp. 129, 120–1, 157.

interpretation, from British official sources, has tended to contract. The National Institute for Economic and Social Research has (no doubt with much help from officials) filled some of the gap with its quarterly *Economic Review*, but this only reaches a small and well-informed section of the public. I have some experience of the problems of interpretation, because for many years past the Ministry of Public Building and Works has released to me certain quarterly building statistics, on which I then write an interpretative article for publication in the journal *Building*. This has caused me to realize, first that the article would be much better if it were written by those who actually compile the statistics, and second that the uninterpreted figures would be exceedingly liable to mislead.

This problem can now be seen, however, as part of a larger one of planning a flow of information. An excess of information (which is a real danger, now that computers have so greatly increased our power to process data) produces mental confusion, delays decision, and probably leads by a process of selection to an exaggeration of unfavourable elements. (This is particularly true where the information is disseminated by the public Press; good news is no news, and our enjoyment of our very real material blessings may be much lessened by the selection of bad news and unfavourable comparisons. How often does the Press remind us that yesterday 99·92 per cent of the working population were *not* on strike?) A nation, like a firm, needs a planned information flow—not too much, but properly interpreted. We have not yet even got to the stage of realizing that late information may be worse than useless, for the Government publishes a considerable mass of statistics which are so long delayed as to be liable to mislead. We still do not think sufficiently hard about the precise purpose for which we want information; we therefore accept what is marginally relevant as though it were fully relevant, and there is insufficient planning to give us exactly what is needed, with the right balance between quality and speed.

The "gold crisis" of 1968 provides an excellent example of the way in which a general sense of misery and impending doom was conveyed to the British public, together with appeals for further sacrifice, on the basis of information which was almost totally irrelevant and (in so far as any was relevant) was unintelligible because it was uninterpreted. Respectable commentators drew parallels with 1931 (and some even threatened us with four million unemployed) without observing that a fundamental difference must exist between a situation in which the United States had a severe deficiency of demand and a situation in which she had an excess of demand. No hypochondriac worrying about his symptoms has ever been sillier.

Let us recall again that the problem suggested by this book is that our use of resources, once minimum subsistence is assured, may fail to improve individual welfare or the state of civilization. This is plainly a problem which goes beyond the division between private and public uses, and it is not going to be solved simply by putting the facts plainly and in a way which directs attention to the real difficulties. What else can be done?

One of the problems of affluence is the tendency to short views (pages 43–50). A man who lives in poverty, as we say "from hand to mouth", necessarily has short views. Greater wealth gives an opportunity for greater foresight, but we do not take this opportunity—partly, no doubt, because of the uncertainty produced by rapid technological change: partly because, though a poor man dare not look to tomorrow, a rich man has no need to— he can let it take care of itself.

Extreme examples of short-sightedness are to be found in Government. When civil servants talk of "long-term planning" they may sometimes be found to have advanced their horizon from six months to three years. Plans which stretch over twenty years are regarded as a waste of time, sure to be wrong, the sort of thing which can safely give an Economic Planning Council something to talk about without any danger of actually influencing policy. In contrast, some industrial firms do make resolute efforts to look well forward; an interesting example was the Unilever twenty-one-year forecast, published as *Britain* 1984. But there is a serious lack of long-term forward thinking, which would have to be a joint concern of industry and Government, about our use of natural resources—and, in consequence, we may, by waste now, put heavy burdens on our successors.

The best way to encourage long-term thinking is to set out and publicize more examples of it. It is an illusion

to suppose that long-run plans are of no use because of
the uncertainty of the future. The appropriate technique
is the *rolling plan*, revised each year (and extended for an
additional year) in the light of the latest estimates.
Guesses about the future are not likely to be wholly right,
but equally they are not likely to be wholly wrong. The
rolling plan provides a possibility of orderly convergence
to the truth, as knowledge increases and the incorrect
elements of information are put right.

A certain large city has a housing shortage and rapidly
increasing population and industry. The immediate official reaction is to look for ways of dealing with the
consequent problems in the short term, that is by finding
peripheral sites on which to build more houses. But a
succession of short-run plans of this sort will produce an
enlargement of urban muddle and mess: the peripheral
development will overload the transport links to the
central area (which was created to deal with a much
smaller population), and land of special value in other
uses will be sacrificed to create housing estates which,
since they are dependent areas governed from a distant
Town Hall, will never be socially satisfactory. The story
is a familiar one: a country rich enough to do first-rate
urban planning in fact produces communities almost as
formless and hideous as those of the nineteenth-century
towns, and destroys its chances of satisfaction by failing
to plan good social units. But put the problems of the
city in their long-run framework. It then becomes
apparent that, allowing for the needs of existing industry
(which is expected to grow), the housing needs of fifteen

or twenty years to come cannot possibly be met in the available peripheral areas. It will be necessary to plan a separate town at a distance, either to act as a dormitory area (with rapid transit links to the existing industry) or as a self-contained unit, attracting some of the industry away from the city. But if this is going to be necessary in twenty years, it may as well start now: the long-term plan shows the hopelessness of a series of short-term expedients, and enables us to get away from muddle to a clear planning principle.

Similarly, three stages of a rolling long-term plan for a region show (a) an expected population increase of around 900,000 in seventeen years: (b) the same increase, but a reduced housing requirement to match it, because it is thought that the average size of household will increase: (c) a reduced population increase (following the Registrar-General's later estimates) of about 750,000, but an unchanged housing requirement, since the heads of households at the terminal date have already been born. These estimates will no doubt fluctuate further as later information comes in, but the conceivable range of fluctuation is limited, and at all points within that range the required number of extra houses considerably exceeds the site provision made in the short-term plans of the authorities in the region. If this situation is allowed to persist, the planning system will break down in a series of unsatisfactory expedients. In this instance also, therefore, the existence of some long-range thinking can help to make the short-term plans consistent, so that they yield greater satisfaction.

These examples are taken from cases where there has been some long-run thinking; but this is relatively rare. Buildings are planned without any clear thought about the cost of their future maintenance. Developments are permitted which in time will affect natural beauty, but it is no one's business to look far ahead and see how the damage can be minimized. Most important of all, there is little forward thinking about the use of the world's natural resources: occasionally disturbing comparisons are published, but they have little effect on policy. This is certainly an area in which the stimulation of further discussion might do valuable service in increasing the long-run satisfaction of humanity.

It is difficult to see how any act of policy can alter the habits of people in trying to "keep up with the Jones's". Copying one's neighbours is not a special vice of the English, but is worldwide. In Britain it is related to all the subtle complications of class-structure—differences of speech and education, job-status, home area, Church and club connexions and so on. Something can perhaps be done by public ridicule of the propensity in its more extreme forms; thus, a series of cartoons in the *Listener* has poked fun at the status symbols of an "in" set of intellectuals. An indirect attack on the stratification of society into groups with similar spending habits can be made by breaking down *other* differences between those groups—for class differences form a mutually supporting system, liable to collapse if support is withdrawn at any point. Some possible areas of attack are—

Differences in methods of payment, between salary earners and wage earners.

Differences in hours of work—"staff" arriving later than "workers", and "management" later still.

Unnecessary privileges for particular groups: the Directors' Dining Room is a sensible privilege, since confidential business may need to be discussed over a meal, but the hierarchy of lavatories for different grades, to be seen in some factories, is less justifiable. Large organizations (including the Civil Service) often have precisely regulated privileges of office furniture, matched to grade; holidays are sometimes related to rank: in fact, the whole system supports the idea that physical attributes go with status.

Encouragement of greater informality, both of dress and of address. We have in fact moved a long way down this path, and in consequence certain forms of imitative expenditure are no longer prevalent; for instance, it is no longer necessary to have special formal dress for Sundays.

An effort to discourage certain social customs which lead to unnecessary expenditure for a purpose which is no longer appropriate or urgent. Examples are the double system of formal evening dress for men and the set pattern of official dinners: such things, by marking the attainment of a particular status, provide rungs on the ladder of spending habits.

But if we must prudently moderate our expectations

of stopping people being snobs, there is surely more to be done in controlling the stimulation of desires (and, particularly, of desires for unnecessary products) by commercial interests. This subject I will discuss at some length under the title of the control of advertising, it being understood that I include in "advertising" all forms of deliberate manipulation or stimulation of demand—for instance, what appear to be news articles in magazines, whose hidden function is to stimulate demand for the products of advertisers in those magazines. I am *not* here concerned with the direct marketing functions of making the qualities of a product known to a potential purchaser, giving technical and after-sales service, and so on: though of course there is no clear line which divides "informative" advertising from that which "manipulates" consumer desires. All those who sell things are, or should be, anxious to do a competent marketing job; the problem here is that the competitive development of marketing may go too far in stimulating unnecessary desire, and thus reducing ultimate satisfaction.

Advertising is a rapidly growing activity: in Britain, the cost is estimated to have grown from £121m in 1948 to £277m in 1955 and £590m in 1965. Part of this increase is accounted for by the general rise in prices, but even after allowing for this the growth rate is six per cent per year.[1] It appears that new media of advertising attract new expenditure without causing serious reduc-

[1] For an excellent survey of the economic effects of advertising, see an article by P. DOYLE, *Economic Journal*, September 1968, from which these figures are taken.

tions in spending on the older media. British expenditure has recently been about 2·7 per cent of the total of consumers' expenditure, as compared with 3·7 per cent in the United States.

It is argued in favour of complete freedom to spend on sales promotion that this activity enables certain producers to obtain a large and stable market, and they can thus pass on the benefits of economies of scale to their customers: that advertising is an open discussion of the quality and performance of rival products, and therefore stimulates technical progress: and that its cost is greatly exaggerated, because as a consequence we get free television and cheaper newspapers. The economies of scale argument is not really a very convincing one, for it is a well-known effect of advertising that it leads to the "differentiation" of products—that is to say, to the introduction of small and often unnecessary variations, designed to attract the attention and loyalty of a particular group of consumers. Furthermore, part of the process of stimulating demand takes the form of fashion changes, intended to make the owners of earlier "models" feel that they are out of date; and frequent fashion changes are not consistent with the economies of long runs of production. Note too that advertising may distract attention from the real differences of quality, and be used as a substitute for price competition, with the result that it confirms and solidifies the shares of the market held by several different producers, instead of allowing one producer to capture the lot and get the full benefits (if such exist) of a large scale of production. Four companies producing similar products, each maintaining a position in the market by advertising in competition with the others, are rather like four countries engaged in an arms race. No one of the competitors can face the cost and risk of the "aggressive action" necessary to win the others' share; but, as long as all are holding the balance by advertising, there is a constant danger of "escalation" —that is to say, of more and more expensive advertising effort (paid for by the consumer) which, since it is matched by all the competitors, leaves the competitive situation just where it was before. It is hard to get from such a situation an argument that advertising *necessarily* yields positive economies to the purchaser, though there may be special cases in which it does so.

In the situation just described, an expensive balance of advertising power constitutes a strong disincentive for new producers to try to break in; they would have not only to meet the costs and risks of pioneering but also to pay for an initial level of promotion sufficient to compete with the loud voices of their rivals. This suggests that advertising might actually impede technical progress. The counter-argument is that it gives firms security, and thus enables them to plan ahead and invest in research and development. In fact, however, technical progress depends on producers being *safe enough but not too safe*; situations of extreme uncertainty are unfavourable, but so are situations of safety, in which comfortable profits can be earned without troubling about the inconvenient incursion of new ideas. There is no presumption that advertising as such creates the ideal balance between security and change. Nor does it seem very sensible to suggest that the stimulation of demand creates technical progress, for the normal sequence is that decisions to produce are taken first, and then efforts are made to sell the product.

As for the argument about cheap newspapers and television, it has no economic respectability whatever. There is no reason to think that people are better off if, when paying for their soap, they are forced to pay a share of their (or someone else's) television as well. On the contrary, there is a presumption that this will produce a misallocation of resources. It is conceivable that cross-subsidization is the only way of providing a free Press—that is to say, that if newspapers cost (say) two shillings no one would buy them. But there is no reason why any necessary subsidy should be a concealed levy on other goods.

Nor must we forget that the association of the "mass media" with advertising tends to lower standards to those that are popular with the largest (and therefore the least educated) groups of buyers—for the wealthy and the educated classes, though they buy more, do not provide a big enough market by themselves to support the most expensive forms of national advertising.

There is not, therefore, in my view much substance in the counter-arguments in favour of complete freedom of advertising and promotional expenditure; and, in the light of the suggestions I have made about its effect on our enjoyment of wealth and on the quality of our civilization, we are free to consider ways of restricting it. This is not easy, for we want—

(a) to allow, and if possible encourage, sensible marketing expenditure which informs purchasers or gives them service:

(b) to be fair as between different media—a tax which bears heavily on one form of advertising is likely simply to divert attention to other forms:

(c) to reduce, or at least not to increase, the advantage which a large producer has because of his ability to engage in massive repetitive advertising—thus raising the initial cost which any small new producer has to bear if he tries to break into the market.

There is no obvious way in which we can segregate for special discouragement expenditure on the stimulation of new and unnecessary desires. It seems sensible, however, to concentrate on the promotion of consumer goods; most of the advertising of these goods is informative, and its relation to the problems discussed here is indirect. Nor could we, without tedious administrative controls, define and segregate expenditure on information. Since what is to be limited is the behaviour of sellers, the burden of any control or tax should rest on them directly; an indirect tax (for instance, on advertising media) is likely to stimulate a search for untaxed forms of marketing expenditure. Furthermore, such a tax, if at a prohibitive rate, would necessarily discourage types of marketing expenditure which are useful; if at a moderate rate, it might be rather easily passed on to the buyer. The determination of advertising appropriations is, after all, a matter of guesswork—no one has yet discovered an accurate method of determining the profitability of advertising, and sellers will be tempted to increase their appropriations by the amount of any tax, because they fear that their rivals will do the same.

Any control will clearly have to be financial. Some kinds of advertising, for instance, newspaper display advertisements (measured in square inches) could be subjected to a control of physical quantity, but this would be very hard to extend to all the varied forms of stimulative promotion. Our search thus leads us to a tax (or the equivalent of a tax), levied on the marketing expenditure of a seller of consumer goods, but with exemption for an initial *tranche* assumed to be required for informative or service work. This, however, does not bring us quite to what we want. Some allowance has to be made for stimulative expenditure by a firm, and particularly a small firm, wishing to break into a market with a new and improved product; this implies that the limit of tax-free expenditure should not be too severe, and should if possible be framed in a way which favours the smaller producer. There is also a danger of diverting effort into wasteful types of packaging and styling, which could be claimed to be production rather than marketing expenditure. This is not a loophole which can be plugged—any restriction of undesirable product variation is likely to bear also on variations which are desirable; but certain steps could be taken to discourage wasteful packaging of products, in the manner suggested below. The details of a restriction on expenditure on the stimulation of consumer demand would require expert study, but the measure might take something like the following form—

(*a*) All expenditure, within the United Kingdom or aimed at the U.K. market, on marketing of every kind (including the cost of staff in the field, the cost of packaging products, and all forms of advertising and promotion) would be disregarded in the computation of profits, unless covered by Marketing Certificates. Disallowance for tax purposes is the equivalent of a substantial tax on the expenditure. Overseas expenditure aimed at foreign markets would remain deductible.

(*b*) Marketing Certificates would be issued (i) on a sliding scale related to turnover—generously on a small turnover, but at smaller proportions as turnover rises: (ii) up to the estimated amount of the raw material content of packaging materials used—that is, excluding the costs of fabricating and printing. Marketing certificates would be transferable, and those with certificates in excess of their actual marketing expenditures could sell the surplus.

(*c*) Marketing expenditure beyond a certain proportion of turnover would be subject to a prohibitive tax (for instance, it might be added three times in the computation of profits). This would be a measure designed to catch the fairly small group of products which have ridiculously high levels of promotion—sometimes in excess of forty per cent of sales value.

It is doubtful if, under this system, it would be necessary

to exempt those who do not sell to final consumers—most of them would have their spending fully covered by marketing certificates. I have outlined a possible plan in some detail, because it illustrates the considerable difficulty and complication of translating, into a suitable measure of control, a theoretical idea that a certain activity, left to itself, will grow to a harmful degree. Any practical policy is likely to be crude and imperfect, and to have some harmful side-effects. If, therefore, a policy can be backed by other assistance, it will be wise to provide it. In this matter of the stimulation of unnecessary demand, the control of "advertising" might be backed up by giving assistance to consumer research and unbiased sources of information for consumers, so as to help to build up resistance to the less rational forms of marketing.

I have several times referred to the dangers which arise from ignoring things, known to be important, because they cannot readily be quantified. There is a logical difficulty here. If I say "It is worth spending money preserving this beautiful piece of country" I may at once be asked "How much money?" If I know the answer, then I have placed a value on the beauty—it has joined the list of quantifiable benefits. If I do not know the answer, I am offering no guide to action. This is why economists show what sometimes seems a perverse desire to charge a price for things, which, as a matter of convenience, have not previously been priced. Recent agitation for "road pricing" is an example.

No doubt more *could* be done. For instance, it would be possible *in theory* to levy a special tax on every visitor entering the Lake District, and by varying this tax to find out something about the price which people are willing to pay for the special qualities of the area. This would still not answer the problem raised in Chapter IX in relation to Manchester's water. For this we require a value for the diminution of enjoyment caused by the impairment of a particular view. It is difficult to see how such a value could ever be found without first spoiling the view; the act of imagination required to set a price on such a change, without ever seeing it, is surely an improbable one. But if it were found (for instance) that a tax of £1 per day corresponded to a certain number of visitors before the change, but that after it the same number of visitors could only be attracted if the tax were 19s., one would at least have an order of magnitude which might then act as a guide in discussing other, hypothetical, changes.

Practical men, however, will rightly revolt against the idea of levying even a simple tax on entry to the area. How does one distinguish the local resident, the person with business in the area, and the person who is passing through to do business (or obtain pleasure) in an adjoining area, from the day tripper or summer visitor? How does one allow for people to visit friends or tend the sick? The interference with freedom involved in even the simplest form of pricing would clearly be very serious, and the administrative burden immense. It would be necessary to have something like the South African system of passes, and to open offices to arrange for the exemption from tax of those who are not visitors. Similar difficulties would certainly arise from any attempt to put a price on other "free" goods.

We must accept, therefore, the fact that a great many benefits will never have a price-tag, and that we ought not to attempt to give them one, because in doing so we would lose other benefits. Professor Mark Blaug, discussing the productivity or efficiency of universities, draws in hard outline the consequent problem—

> It is logically impossible to argue both that the objectives of universities are non-quantifiable and that the universities are now achieving these objectives more successfully. This is not to assert that "what is not measurable is not significant", but rather that when decisions have to be taken in terms of "more or less", resort to the unspecified social, ethical and spiritual contributions that universities make to society is simply designed to take the question out of the realm of rational discourse.[1]

Unfortunately the basing of decisions on the things which *can* be quantified has only a formal rationality. It is as though a man were to say "In interpreting the letters and instructions I receive, I shall ignore all words of less than four letters." The remaining words might on occasion yield an intelligible message, but it might well be the wrong one (for instance, by the omission of the word "not").

I doubt, however, if the problem is quite as bad as it

[1] Address to Universities' Conference, Spring 1968.

looks. If we say that something cannot be *measured*, the image in the mind is that of a foot rule or tape measure, which tells us that *A* is two inches long and *B* is four inches long, and consequently *B* is twice as long as *A*. But there are other statements about quantity which are not of this kind. For instance, the assertion that the scent of this rose is *stronger* than the scent of that is perfectly meaningful, although the speaker has in mind no scale on which the strength of a scent can be measured, and it is in fact not easy to devise one. We often make statements about things being "better" or "more important" without having any clear idea of magnitude. Even in such examples, however, introspection may suggest a rough classification into groups, which constitutes a kind of approximate measurement. For instance, we can look at the buildings around us, and classify some as "of the highest importance", "priceless", "worth keeping at almost any cost": another group will be "important", "valuable", "worth maintaining" (though with an implicit limit on cost): another group will be "good", and we note that we should think carefully before allowing demolition or change: while others will be "of no great importance" and we take no special steps to preserve them. A classification rather like this is in fact used for buildings of historic and architectural importance. It may still need an arbitrary decision to put values against the various classes—for instance, to say that we would be willing to spend £1m to keep a building in the first group, £20,000 for one in the second, £5,000 for one in the third, and nothing for a building in the fourth group. But it will be better to use such a rough classification, and such arbitrary values, where we have to, rather than to ignore all differences of beauty or architectural merit because we have no means of measuring them accurately.

The danger which we have seen to face an affluent society is that of giving too much attention to benefits which are easily measured in money, and thereby putting in danger qualities of civilization which have no readily determined money value. The essential point, therefore, is to list all the factors which seem of importance, in relation to a particular decision, and then to seek some way (however approximate) of bringing them all into the balance, instead of concentrating, as we very readily do, on those which have firm numbers attached to them. Wise and experienced men sometimes get a bad reputation with the young, because their pronouncements lack exactitude. This, however, may be a sign of their wisdom rather than their senility; when they talk about "judgements" and "hunches", they are bringing into their decisions the less quantifiable factors, about which only vague verbal statements can be made. But this does not necessarily make the decisions worse, and may make them much better. A man does not usually decide to marry a wife solely because of her dowry, or her vital statistics; other factors, of a type distinctly difficult to quantify, enter in.

At this point, the reader may feel like lodging a modest complaint. Here are certain dangers set before us: a society which is rich but not happy, which has the means of civilized achievement but does not advance in quality. To stop this, rather fundamental, rot we have so far been offered some remarks about growth as an object of policy: an argument which favours the fixing of a subsistence level, and some conscious thought about the use of the surplus: some remarks about the improvement of the flow of information: a plea for long-term thinking about the use of resources: some lines of attack on social snobbery: a plan for a marketing tax: a suggestion about the attitude to matters not readily quantifiable. This is an odd mixture of vague hopes and precise proposals, and it does not add up to a policy. But this, I think, is an inevitable problem. There are a few specific things which might help us to attain a saner appreciation of Wealth, but for the most part what is needed is a change of attitudes which will then inform both public policy and individual action. This change can only be stated in rather broad terms, and the means of bringing it about is not by passing Acts of Parliament, but by getting people to talk about it. That is why this book was written.

The change of attitude means, I think, a lessening of the pretensions of economists, but an improvement of their status. Paradoxically, economics is now powerful, but commands little esteem. Whereas the layman does not feel competent to discuss the problems of nuclear physics, he has no inhibitions about the discussion of economic problems, even if they really require considerable technical knowledge. (Indeed, it is noticeable that eminent scientists frequently consider themselves competent to discuss economic problems.) The professional economist is regarded as a man who has nothing definite to say, or (if he attempts a definite pronouncement) is capable of immediate nullification by quoting an opposite opinion from another professional economist. Public attitudes are often embalmed in jokes. There is the employer who advertised for a one-armed economist, and, on being asked the reason why, said: "We had one of those fellows before, and he was always saying 'On the one hand, this . . . On the other, that . . .' " There is the story of the examiner who set the same economics paper two years running, and justified it by saying "Ah, but you see *we* change the answers". Where two economists meet, we are told, there will be three opinions. The disasters of Government economic policy are frequently blamed on the poor quality of their professional advice, but the public does not consider that there are other professionals who would be better; "plain, ordinary men" or "good business men" are thought to be the right people to put things in order.

Yet the rather limited outlook of professional economists, as outlined in Chapter II, has exercised a powerful influence on the conventional wisdom of the age. More wealth is always a good thing: what cannot be valued in money is unimportant: since there is no exact way of relating wealth to happiness or the quality of civilization, ignore the relation. Indeed, the very definition which is supposed to limit the field of interest of economics and thus assert the importance of other things—namely, that economics is concerned with things which can be brought into relation with the measuring-rod of money—is assimilated into the conventional wisdom as though it said that only what is measured in money is important. Those who fight for a purpose not readily valued in money are met by the question "Is it *worth* it?" By asking the wrong question, a materialist society ensures that it will not have achievements which match its resources.

I would like to see economists, therefore, kept in their place, but in that place honoured as competent professionals. The richer a country becomes, the less need it has to be ruled by economic thinking, and the more it should turn its attention to what Keynes, in the passage quoted in the Preface, called "other matters of greater and more permanent significance". Unlicensed economists will never be as easily suppressed as unlicensed dentists, but perhaps if the economist is seen as a technician rather than a main pillar of society he may win the esteem which is given to the humble, competent dentist.

The change of public attitudes to economics, however, can occur as a consequence of a wider change, but hardly as the main cause of that change. Our failure to get satisfaction from wealth is a consequence of regarding it as too important; therefore other purposes must be emphasized. Some of the worldwide movements among young people amount to a total rejection of the values of a materialist society, but it is evident that it is hard to find an appropriate alternative. Are we to recommend devotion to personal happiness, following William Penn's advice?—

Seek not to be rich but happy. The one lies in bags, the other in content; which wealth can never give. If thou wouldst be happy bring thy mind to thy condition, and have an indifferency for more than what is sufficient. Have but little to do, and do it thyself. And do to others as thou wouldst have them do to thee. So thou canst not fail of temporal felicity.[1]

The difficulty about this advice is that it can easily lead to an attitude which forgets society in its concentration on the individual, and thus in time reacts back unfavourably on the individual. Furthermore, a purpose beyond happiness is needed: dedication to fulness of personal experience can become a degrading form of self-indulgence. Many a heroin addict began by seeking an escape into personal happiness. Some would wish us to set up a devotion to the creative arts as the great purpose of mankind. But neither beauty nor self-expression are all-inclusive and sufficient aims; nor is this attitude alone likely to be effective, for the materialist society is highly efficient in establishing low and uniform standards of taste and in discouraging individual creativity. I would myself doubt whether we can put Wealth in its right place without a major rediscovery of man as a spiritual being—that is, if you like, without a religious revival, though I have little idea with what form of religion the revival might be concerned. What I consider essential is the belief in self-fulfilment, and in advance to a higher level of achievement, through co-operation with or

[1] This quotation, like that on page 170 below, comes from *Some Fruits of Solitude*.

union with a greater universal purpose. Those who cannot accept this belief will, I think, find it hard to suggest a way in which we can avoid being mastered by our own affluence. For I return, at the end, to William Penn—

Such now is become our delicacy, that we will not eat ordinary meat, nor drink small, palled liquor; we must have the best and the best cooked for our bodies, while our souls feed on empty or corrupted things. In short, man is spending all upon a bare house, and hath little or no furniture within to recommend it; which is preferring the cabinet before the jewel, a lease of seven years before an inheritance. So absurd a thing is man, after all his proud pretences to wit and understanding.

BIBLIOGRAPHY

THE reader will see that there is not much published which directly follows the line of this book. I therefore append an alphabetical list of books which have certainly influenced what it contains, and which may be helpful to others.

BRECH, R., *Britain 1984* (Humanities Press, 1963).

DUESENBERRY, J. S., *Income, Saving and the Theory of Consumer Behaviour* (Harvard, 1949).

GALBRAITH, J. K., *The Affluent Society* (Houghton Mifflin, 1958).

GALBRAITH, J. K., *The Liberal Hour* (Houghton Mifflin, 1960).

HARROD, R. F., *The Life of John Maynard Keynes* (Macmillan, 1951).

HAWTREY, R. G., *The Economic Problem* (Longmans, 1926).

KATONA, G., *Psychological Analysis of Economic Behavior* (McGraw Hill, 1951).

KEYNES, J. M., *Essays in Persuasion* (Macmillan, 1961).

LITTLE, I. M. D., *A Critique of Welfare Economics* (Oxford, 1960).

MARSHALL, A., *Principles of Economics* (Ed. C. W. Guillebaud) (Macmillan, 1961).

MAYER, M. P., *Madison Avenue U.S.A.* (Penguin, 1961).

MILL, J. S., *Principles of Political Economy* (Longmans Green, 1878 edn.)

MORGAN, E. V., *The Structure of Property Ownership in Great Britain* (Oxford, 1960).

PACKARD, V., *The Hidden Persuaders* (McKay, 1957).

PACKARD, V., *The Status Seekers* (McKay, 1959).

PACKARD, V., *The Waste Makers* (McKay, 1961).

PIGOU, A. C., *The Economics of Welfare* (4th ed.) (Macmillan, 1938).

ROBERTSON, D. H., *Lectures on Economic Principles* (Fontana, 1963).

ROWNTREE, B. S., *Poverty: a Study of Town Life* (Macmillan, 1901).

ROWNTREE, B. S., *Poverty and Progress* (Longmans, 1941).

ROWNTREE, B. S., and LAVERS, G. R., *Poverty and the Welfare State* (Longmans, 1951).

SMILES, S., *Self-Help* (Centenary edition) (Murray, 1958).

SMITH, A., *The Wealth of Nations* (Ed. McCulloch) (Black, 1863 edn.).

SHACKLE, G. L. S., *Economics for Pleasure* (Cambridge, 1959).

SHACKLE, G. L. S., *Decision, Order and Time* (Cambridge, 1961).

SHACKLE, G. L. S. (Ed.), *A New Prospect of Economics* (Harcourt, Brace, 1958).

INDEX